Never Alone

By
Gayle Garcia
with Joshua Weber

GRG Publishing

Gayle Garcia
Winchester, CA 92596
Layout and design by RAZ Productions, Studio City, CA.

Printed in the United States of America
First Printing: May 2015

Dedication

To anyone who has ever felt alone

SECTIONS

Foreword

by Pastor Bret Mileski & Lucinda Mileski
The Rock Church, Temecula Valley

Hope, faith, love and victory! That's what this book reveals. We hear, too many times, the tragedy of a child who, whether out of loss, confusion or desperation, stumbles down the path of addiction, only to be overwhelmed, taken over and forever lost to it.

This is not that story. Through a mother's tenacious, unwavering faith and love, and by the grace and mercy of God, we see His plan unfold in a powerful and beautiful way.

I've known Gayle for many years, believed and prayed with her. Not once did she underestimate God or His promises.

She never let go of her boy, regardless of the circumstances, what people said, the trials or even the darkness that seemed endless when glancing toward the end of the tunnel. The great message of this story is that **God never lets go either!**

There were many times when Gayle wasn't sure she should write this book. She prayed, waited, and then, thankfully, answered the call. I'm so glad she did. Throughout this journey I was privileged, as a friend, to witness little glimpses of God's hand along the way. It was such a blessing to see what He was doing. But now we get to be a part of the miracle. Reading this book, I didn't feel like a mere spectator. I felt like I was traveling the road with Gayle and Joshua. Their setbacks were my setbacks and their victories were mine as well.

This book had to be written. When God moves in this way, when He rescues, restores and transforms, the world needs to hear about it.

1

I was deeply moved and forever changed by this story. Through Gayle and Joshua's journey, their bravery and commitment, my faith was rekindled and I was reminded, once again, that no matter how ominous or futile life can seem, we should never buy the lie that there is no hope. Never let go but fight the battle as they did, on their knees.

Thank you, Gayle and Joshua for illuminating the astounding truth that we are **Never Alone.**

Introduction

My name is Gayle Garcia and I am Joshua's mom. This story is about our journey of, first tragedy and despair, and ultimately, of hope. I thought I should give you some background information, so let me start with this:

I was married really young, at age 18. By the time I was 22, I was a single mother with a 3 year old (my Daughter) and a 1 year old (Joshua) and had no job skills or education. I didn't even have a high school diploma. (Yes, I eventually went back to school and got my GED.) I had no visible means of support and it stayed that way for several years. My kids and I lived with my parents even after I went to work.

I started out working at a fast food restaurant and then took a second job as a night cashier at a gas station. It was horrible. I hardly ever got to see my children, but once I had cash-handling experience, I was able to get a job as a teller in a bank. With this, things improved, but only slightly. At least now I was working a set schedule of Monday through Friday, 8 to 5, and had medical insurance, but not much salary. I was able to move my kids and myself into our own place, but I struggled to pay the rent, buy groceries, and provide the bare basics for the three of us. Still, things weren't all bad. My kids and I always had a lot of fun. We went camping with my parents and I took them to the beach in the summer to play in the surf, and to the mountains in the winter to play in the snow. We picked apples every fall and spent the holidays with our extended family. We also attended church together.

I never regretted having children. I did regret that I was often so tired from working all day that I was sometimes impatient with them. It was hard to work all day, try to figure out how to pay the bills, and stay up late at night cleaning and doing laundry while they slept.

There were also times when, if we hadn't eaten dinner with my parents, we wouldn't have had any dinner at all. I can remember crying one winter because I didn't have enough money to buy my kids new coats. The one saving grace was that we lived in California; even the coldest day isn't really all that cold compared to most other states. I remember how excited I was when I went to a discount store in town and found down jackets for $10.00 each! I bought a lavender one for my daughter and a dark blue one for Joshua. And then, I smiled for the rest of the day.

As I began to work my way up in the banking industry, our situation improved. By the time my daughter was in middle school, things were better. I was at a job where I was allowed to work overtime--it helped cover the extra expenses. I was able to pay for horseback riding lessons for her, as well as signing Joshua up for sports. We were still pretty poor, but we had moved to an apartment in a safer part of town and could actually eat dinner at home most nights. I could only afford a two bedroom place, so I gave each child their own room while I slept on a hide-a-bed couch in the living room. By the time my daughter was in high school, I was able to pay for her to go through drivers training and go to prom and Joshua got his own dirt bike! He and I went to the desert one weekend with my brother and his family so he could ride. We were only able to go that one time, but better once then never!

I tried to date. I tried getting married again too. It didn't work out. I didn't seem to be very good at picking men. I really thought my marriage was going to be a good match. This man attended church, we both loved sports and he seemed to be willing to accept my teenage children. What I envisioned is not at all what it turned out to be. I think some of Joshua's troubles may have stemmed from the hurt and frustration he felt over not having a Dad. Then, when he thought that we had found someone to fill that void, the rejection he faced from this man may have been more than he could handle.

I am not a psychologist, or very knowledgeable in those matters, but I do remember how painful the rejection was for Joshua. On our first Christmas as a family, Joshua took his allowance and bought a gift for this man. He attached a card to it that said, "To my new Dad". His "new Dad" never responded--not a word, not even a simple thank you. The silence, for Joshua, I'm sure, was deafening. For me, it was extremely disappointing. I realized not only did the man I had married not love me, but he had also emotionally damaged my child. It was at that point I left the marriage. It took no time at all (we hadn't even filed for divorce yet) for this man to move on to someone else. (As for me, I did finally marry someone who not only loved me deeply, but someone who also loved my children. He is a Father to them in every way my previous husband had not been. I had known this man for years; he had watched my children grow up. Loving us seemed to come naturally to him. After all of the tears and heartbreak, my kids and I had finally found love. Although it was after my children were adults, healing came to our family by way of this man's gentle love for us, and it continues on to the present day.)

Now, back to our story. When Joshua was in his early teens, he began acting out. This brilliant child, who had been an ace student, began getting into trouble at school. I was receiving constant calls from his teachers and other school officials regarding his behavior. It appeared that the only time Joshua got any attention from his (previous) Step-Dad was when he was in trouble. Although I did my best to handle this new situation, I was, as I'm sure most parents are, ill equipped. Was this what started Joshua's downward spiral? As his Mother, on the outside looking in, it seemed very likely.

After a few years of trying and failing to turn Joshua around, he was arrested. It was 1998; he was 15 years old. Thirteen years and many tears later, Joshua was arrested for the final time. Not knowing that it would be his final arrest, I steeled myself for what lay ahead:

the visits to county jail, the court dates and the phone calls that would inevitably come. I was exhausted and unsure that I could weather another term of Joshua being incarcerated.

I asked God for his peace and wisdom. He spoke to me through my quiet time with him. His answer was simple, "Stand by your son. Never leave him alone. He's coming home to you one day." I mustered up my courage and prepared myself for the misunderstandings and criticism that I would ultimately face, knowing that I would not be able to explain why I had chosen this road… and finally understanding that I really didn't need to explain it at all.

The Beginning of the End

The Arrest and County Jail

On May 19, 2011 at 1:30am, my son Joshua was arrested for Driving Under the Influence. Sadly, this was just the latest in a string of DUI arrests and convictions; at this point, I had lost count of exactly how many arrests and convictions. Joshua was so heavily addicted to drugs and alcohol that his life had become a revolving door of going in-and-out of first county jail, and then state prison.

It wasn't always that way. There were earlier years in his life when teachers, pastors, friends, and family saw something different in Joshua--something special. He was funny and smart, a natural leader whom other children instinctively followed. And was he ever cute! Joshua was a strawberry blonde with green eyes and a sprinkle of freckles across his nose. He was born on his due date. I'm sure there are other children who were born on their due dates; I have never personally known any... only my Joshua, weighing 6 pounds 15 ounces. Such is the shape of a Mother's heart; it never forgets. It always treasures. Joshua and I were both going to need that unconditional love in the years that followed.

It was hard to believe that my "Little Buddy" had grown up to be something entirely different from what I had expected. However, there were still moments when he (the "Real Joshua") would stand up and be heard, only to sink back down into the terrible spiral that his life had become.

Joshua was first arrested in December of 1998 when he was 15 years old. I got a call from the local police department to come and pick him up from their station. My first reaction was disbelief. I was convinced there must have been some kind of mistake. As I listened to the officer on the other end of the phone, the reality of what was happening began to slowly sink in. I felt as if I had been kicked in the stomach. I was shaking and crying and almost vomited. How could this have happened? Joshua was well-liked among his peers, a good student, and a genuinely sweet boy. How could he have been arrested? I had to stay calm enough to be able to get into the car and pick him up. When I saw him, I didn't know what to say. I lost my temper and handled the situation poorly. I was so out of my mind that I was unable to properly parent him. This was one of the important lessons that God was going to teach me over the next 15 years and one that Joshua would give me plenty of opportunities to learn.

"Using" Again

In 2011, just prior to his most recent arrest, Joshua came by our house to visit me on Mother's Day. Even in his drug altered state, he remembered that it was Mother's Day. Joshua knows love; he just doesn't always choose it. In the weeks leading up to his arrest I had taken note of a significant drop in his weight and a change in his attitude. He was surly and belligerent. I privately told my husband that he didn't look good and that he was acting like he was "using" again. When Josh went to leave, I walked out with him. I made sure to look into his eyes and tell him that I loved him. He stared back at me with that vacant look. He was definitely using again.

Just 11 days later, Joshua was arrested. My Mom called me a little after 4am and said that he had called her collect and that he was in county jail. (I only have a cell phone so he wasn't able to call me collect.) He wanted us to go pick up his truck. My heart sank as I thought, "Not again." Joshua had been out of prison for less than a year; he was a few weeks away from being off of parole. He had a good paying job and a new truck. Now he would lose all that. We couldn't afford to bail him out and if he couldn't get out of jail to get to work, well… that would be the end of the progress he had made while sober.

I dreaded the thought of rushing down from my home in Riverside County to San Diego County where Joshua had been arrested, especially during morning rush hour traffic. I had been through this so many times before; how was I going to deal with it one more time? I let my Mom know that I would be down later that day. I tried to go back to sleep, but of course I couldn't. My mind was racing; my stomach was upset and my heart was broken, so I got up, drank some coffee, showered and made the 45-minute trip to my Mother's house.

Upon arrival, my Mom told me that Joshua's truck was in the parking lot of a bar close to where he had been arrested. He wanted us to go get it so it wouldn't be towed and impounded by the police. At this point, Joshua was still hoping he could salvage the pieces of his life and put them back together. He was desperate and grasping at straws.

We climbed into my Mother's car and made the short drive to where the truck was located. We found it easily enough; there were only a few other cars in the lot. I unlocked the truck with the extra set of keys and opened the door. I was nearly knocked over by the stench of alcohol. I noticed that the floor was littered with empty mini bottles of booze as well as full bottles of hard liquor and cans of beer. I gathered them all up (full and empty) and carried them to the nearest trash can to throw them away. We would be taking surface streets back to my Mom's house. It would be an easier drive for her rather than taking the freeway. We eventually took the truck to my house in Riverside County and later turned it in to the bank that held the loan. They sold it, paid off what they could and charged the rest of the balance to Joshua.

After I returned home, I went online to look Joshua up on the jail website. I wanted to see where he was being held and what he was being charged with. In doing so, I found out that I could email Joshua through the jail website. This is how our written communication to one another began.

Everyday Things

On May 20, 2011 I sent my first email to Joshua:

> *Hi Josh,*
> *Hope you are hanging in there. Hope you are feeling OK.*
> *I went to Wal-Mart today and bought some watermelon,*
> *cantaloupe, onions and tomatoes for a garden. I guess*
> *Fino* [my husband] *and I will plant them all this weekend*
> *over on the side of the house by the dining room window.*

*Hopefully, the "Snail Brigade" won't eat them all. I
swear I have never seen so many snails in one place
in my whole life as there are at this house. So gross!
I have talked with Chris [Joshua's boss and friend]
several times to try to take care of your responsibili-
ties, the van and your truck payment in particular. I will
put some money on the jail spending account for you. I
just have to figure out how to do it. Keep me posted on
what's going on. Stay calm. Love, Mom*

It seems strange now to think that I was writing to him about gar-
dening, but he always liked to hear about things on the outside. It
made him feel more normal and took his mind off of his circumstances. I talked with him on the phone earlier in the day; he was
distraught over his situation. He was devastated by the foolishness
of his behavior and by all that he had lost: his job, his truck, and
most importantly, his freedom. I knew he was very disappointed,
but what I didn't know is that he was "drug sick" from coming down
off of heroin. In the years leading up to this latest arrest, Joshua
struggled with heroin addiction. He stayed at my home more than
once to try to kick this terrible drug. I guess somewhere deep within
him was the desire to fight the addiction. The pull to try it "just one
more time" seemed to always win the battle. Once, I woke up in the
middle of the night and sat straight up in bed. I was having a vision
(or something) of Joshua lying on a pile of rags. He was dying. I was
so afraid. I began to pray. I rocked back and forth, sang praises and
prayed. I prayed until the sun came up. I had to get ready for work
and while doing so I continued to pray. I prayed for my son's life. I
prayed for his mind to be protected. I prayed for his spirit to remain
intact. I prayed all day and into the night.

A few days later, Joshua came home. It must have been a Saturday,
because I remember that I didn't have to work. I was so relieved
when I heard Joshua open the door and go into his bedroom that
I immediately began thanking God for his safe return. At that moment, I felt that God was impressing upon me to go and talk to
Joshua. I was reluctant, but when God tells you to do something, it's

always best to obey. I walked down the hallway towards Joshua's bedroom. I knocked softly on the door and listened for a response. None came. Slowly and quietly I turned the door knob and opened the door. Joshua was lying on his bed with his back to me. I sat down in the chair directly across from him, mustered up my nerve and softly spoke. I told him about the vision I had of him lying on the rags dying and said, "I don't know what you are using, but if you don't stop, you are going to die." Without rolling over he snarled, "Get out of my room," so I did. I left him lying there and as I exhaled said, "OK Lord, the rest is up to you." I'm not sure how much time passed, but once Josh was able to get out of bed, he came to me and said, "Mom." When I heard his "I need your help" voice, I knew he was going to tell me something I didn't want to hear. I was standing at the sink washing dishes. (Seems every time something happened with Joshua, I was at the sink washing dishes.) I turned around slowly and asked, "Yes?" Hesitantly he replied, "It was real." I was perplexed and asked, "What was real?" He said, "It wasn't a vision. It was real, only I wasn't lying on a pile of rags. It was an old beat-up chair." I felt the hair on my arms stand up. He continued, "I was using so much, and the guy I was with kept shooting me up with more and more drugs. I started to die. My spirit left my body and was up by the ceiling looking down on myself. All of my senses were heightened: sound, smell. All I could do was hang-on."

I could barely believe what I was hearing. God had awakened me in the middle of night, so I would pray for my son, so He could save his life! Joshua put out his fisted hand, opened it and showed me several used hypodermic needles. I was stunned and frightened, but knew that if I was going to help him, I had to stay calm. I waited until Joshua said, "I need you to take me to a place where I can safely throw these away. I want to know if it's OK for me to stay here with you while I kick drugs." My heart reached out to my son and I said, "Yes." I told Josh to go shower and we would go right away to get rid of the needles. I drove him to the local hospital where he threw the needles in the biohazard trash can. He went by himself and when he got back into the car he said, " You should have seen the way the lady looked at me, Mom" and his head dropped down. I felt so bad for him, but also knew that it was a harsh reality check and he needed to face it. I softened my voice and said, "I know; but Joshua, she knows what you have been doing and people aren't OK with it." He nodded, but did not speak. For the next 3 weeks I watched as my beautiful boy went through the agony of heroin withdrawal. He couldn't eat or sleep. He couldn't lie down or sit up. He vomited constantly. At first it was food that was coming up, but in an effort to stop the vomiting, he stopped eating. Even after that, he would throw up disgusting brown stuff, and then stomach bile until nothing was left to vomit and he would dry heave for hours. He would sweat and then get chills. His muscles hurt. He said that even his hair hurt. He was in so much pain at one point, I pleaded with him to tell me if he needed to be taken to the hospital. He was so sick he could barely answer; he just shook his head from side to side.

And finally, he was clean. I have heard it said, "Nobody wants to grow up to be a drug addict." After watching Joshua kick heroin cold turkey, I knew that was true.

County Lock Up

A New Pair of Shoes

In the days that followed Joshua's arrest, I wrote several more emails to him.

May 21, 2011

Dear Josh,
Once again, hang on. It's a strange, dark journey, but it can be navigated and accomplished. Teresa's daughter, Noel (remember her?), has cancer. She has to have chemotherapy. Her beautiful, thick hair is going to fall out. She will vomit most days and on other days be too weak to eat. She will be too tired to hold her husband or to care for her daughter, and too tired to sing. Is that worse than what you face? That's hard to judge. Pain and darkness feel the same no matter the package they're wrapped in, so hang on.

Even if it is in things unseen, you can choose hope. You can get up in the morning and put it on like a new pair of shoes and wear it all day long. You can get it from other people and give it away. Hope is a song, or the sound of birds coming across the wire. It's a sliver of light in the darkness that cannot, will not, be overtaken. Have hope and in a time such as this, know that you are loved.
Love, Mom

After reading this email message, Joshua shared with me via a collect phone call that he got out of bed for the first time in 5 days. I sent an email to Noel's Mother, my worship pastor, to let her know that Joshua was inspired by Noel's story. (Noel is a beautiful, young wife and Mother who attends my church and sings on the worship team).

NOEL'S SONG

The worship she brings to each day is not only carried on chords of music. Her life is a song of hope. The iron [strength] that God is building in her is lovelier than the finest gold. Her story reached into the darkest place--to Joshua, in jail, sick from heroin withdrawals. He read the story of Noel's life and chose hope. He said he "put hope on like a new pair of shoes." For the first time in 5 days, he got out of bed. He ate. He read his Bible. He wrote a letter. He called and asked me to tell you how sorry he is that Noel is going through such a hard thing. He always found her beautiful.

Her song, her name, her faith, her God, they pierced the darkness, laid flat the enemy and gave hope in a place where hopelessness resides. Against all odds, her story spoke to the heart of a prisoner, and where there should be none, brought hope.

God is on Your Side

May 23, 2011

Dear Josh,
I am going to try to visit you on Thursday the 26th or Sunday the 29th. I can schedule a visit online so I will do that as soon as the web link opens up on Tuesday. Do you know the story of Joseph (from the Bible)? His brothers sold him into slavery. Nice guys, huh? Then,

someone told a lie and he ended up in jail. He worked in the jail for 12 years. He spoke about God and interpreted the prisoners' dreams. When the Pharaoh had a dream he did not understand, one of the prison guards told him about Joseph.

The Pharaoh called Joseph to him. Joseph explained the dream. The Pharaoh was so impressed that he got Joseph out of jail and eventually made him 2nd in command over the entire kingdom. During a famine, Joseph's brothers travelled to Egypt to trade their belongings for food. They didn't know that Joseph was there. When they were brought before him, they didn't recognize him, but he knew who they were. He called them to him. He cried and hugged them. He forgave them. They were ashamed and filled with regret, because they sold him into slavery. Joseph took care of them for the rest of their lives. What man meant for harm, God used for good.

Never forget the miracles!

Don't forget who is on your side. I am on your side. Fino is on your side. We will always be here for you, but most importantly, God is on your side; and if God is on your side what does it matter who is against you or what you are up against?
Love, Mom

Many years back, I told Joshua about a dream I had. Angels and demons were flying in the sky above me waging war. The buildings surrounding me were destroyed. Smoke and ash filled the air. There was screaming and crying. It was the end of the world. I was trying to find my children. They were lost. It was so real and frightening that I woke up shaking and scared. It changed my life completely.

Trust God

May 24, 2011

Hi Josh,
I think the hardest thing I have ever had to deal with as
a person is being misunderstood. When I had the dream
about the angels and demons, it completely changed my
life. From that point forward, I began making deci-
sions based on Biblical principles and what I felt God,
through prayer, was telling me. No one understood.
They were treating me like I was the same old Gayle I
had always been, but I was different. People criticized,
ridiculed and gossiped about me. People I should have
been able to trust were not acting in a trustworthy way.
It hurt, but I had a confidence that whether or not they
understood, God was guiding me and because of that,
I knew that I could withstand whatever was leveled
against me.

I had to move forward, taking every step in line with
what the Bible says is right. I made a few mistakes,
but the longer I walked with God, the better my judg-
ment became. People began to see that I was acting
and working in a new way, with new convictions. I was
strong and sure. I didn't argue or involve myself in
wrong doings. Eventually, the very people who criti-
cized and judged me came to respect me; or knowing
they could not goad me into arguing or playing their
games, they left me alone. Now I lead a ministry. I still
make mistakes, but I am at a much higher level of man-
agement and carry a much heavier burden. To whom
much is given, much is required. But, I still use the same
basic principles.

Read the Bible every day. Obey Gods word. Apply it to life
situations, and pray. It will work for you too. Trust me. No
wait... trust God. :) Love, Mom

An email sent to my Pastor on May 27, 2011. He had asked me to keep
him updated on Joshua's situation so that he could pray for him. I had
spoken with him about Joshua many times. Not all the conversations
were pleasant... or easy.

Hello,
First of all, we missed you terribly. It just wasn't the same
church without your energy and enthusiasm. And sec-
ondly, let me update you about Joshua. I never told him
about any of the conversations that we had about him. I
never told him that you were praying for him or that you
said you saw things in the spirit regarding his anger and
pain... and his sweetness. I never shared with him about
how you shaved off your sideburn in error, because of the
battle for his soul. Until today, I kept those things from
him because it seemed like the right thing to do. I held
onto them, not willing to use them until the timing was
right, wondering if it was ever going to be.

I guess you are now suspecting that something has
changed. You are right. He is in jail and that's a good
thing. He was arrested a week ago Wednesday for driving
under the influence. He was using heroin, cocaine and
who knows what else. He said he was using so much at
one time that he was almost overdosing. Had he not been
arrested, he may have died... or killed someone else. As it
is, God's mighty hand, once again, reached into his situ-
ation and spared him. He is like Jonah in the belly of the
whale. He is being set free by becoming a prisoner. Isn't
that just like God?

Joshua is pressing into God like I have never seen him before. Even as I doubt, I rejoice. I told him to not only call out for the hand of God to rescue him, but to also obey and be in a relationship with God before the crisis hits. He talked to me about 1 Corinthians 13 and said, "Mom, it's this scripture and it's all about love. I remember you telling it to me. In another place the scriptures says that when you're a kid, you act like a kid, but when you become a man, you have to stop acting like a kid. I remember you telling me that one too. They are starting to make sense to me Mom." It reminded me of a friend telling me that nothing you do for God returns void. God imprinted the scriptures on my son's heart, and now they are changing him. I told Pastor Bret about Josh's sudden change and expressed my concern that it would be short lived. He reminded me that the Father never questioned the prodigal son, he just welcomed him home. That's a good word.

Today, I told Josh that he should write to you. He said he would like that and asked if you would write to him. He wanted me to give you his (temporary) address. I told him about you praying for him and about your sideburn. Josh laughed about the sideburn. I laughed with him. It was sort of funny. (Maybe not for you.) Anyway, here is his address for now. He will be sentenced on June 16th. It looks like he is going to serve 2 ½ years in fire camp. He's gotta face the penalty for his crime. Better that than lose him for good.

I know you are super busy, so if you don't get time to write, I understand. But if you do have the chance, he would be pleased. Thank you for your prayers. They helped save my son. Love, Gayle

⊷⊶

This is Joshua's first letter since being arrested. It was written to a
young woman he had been dating at the time. He was sorry that he
had lost that relationship along with everything else.

May 29, 2011

Dear Amanda,
This isn't going to be a very handsome letter. The least
amount of time that I can get is 32 months at 80%, which
turns out to be around 26 months. Not that I think you
care, but I figure I might as well let you know since you
were with me when it all went down. Here are a few things
I would say to you as a friend, before I get to what's really
on my mind. I know you're smart and you can see for
yourself, but the thing about you and that girl hanging out
(not that I'm bagging on her), I'm not sure that's such a
good idea. She's a tweeker and the people she hangs with
aren't much different. I'm just saying. It's your life and
you can do what you wish.

So I must admit, I'm not sure why you are not accepting
my calls or writing to me…? But I'm feeling pretty used
and hurt. All I ever wanted from you was your honesty
and your friendship. I used to think that you had the abil-
ity to care; now I'm beginning to doubt that you ever did.
Maybe I was just a free ride. But don't you fret none, Lil'
Miss, I enjoyed the time I shared with you, even if it was
only for a moment.

However, on the contrary, I understand that you're 21,
good looking, just got out of a relationship and you want
to go see what life has to offer and be free and wild.

That's absolutely understandable. But let me say this as someone who knows the value of friendship... the next time you meet someone like me: someone that has a huge heart, open arms and a shoulder to cry on, as well as will go out of their way for you, do whatever it takes to see you smile, would always forgive you, and be someone that genuinely cares... I would say to you, capture it and hold that person dear and close, because good friends are very few and far between. I know. I can count my true friends on one hand. They're the ones who were there before, and will be there during, and will be waiting with loving arms after my incarceration. Please don't think this is a good-bye letter. I'm just writing down how I'm feeling. I would love nothing more than to hear from you. It's always nice to hear from a friend. The ball is in your court.

He never finished the letter.

Joshua had asked me to go to this young woman's house and pick up some items he had left there. When I called to make arrangements, the young woman was belligerent and rude. She even used bad language while speaking with me. I have to say that I wasn't upset that this relationship did not stand the test of time.

No Wonder I'm Tired

May 30, 2011

Hi Josh,
Hope you're doing OK. Louie [his dog] is adjusting to life at our house. He is a bit stubborn, but learns really fast. He likes being good and getting loves and treats. He is a very sweet dog. I feel better knowing that he is here and not all alone. He is a people person...

or people dog. We are going to your sister's house on
Wednesday for your nephew's birthday. He is 11 now. I
bought him a Star Wars Lego set. It came with C3PO,
R2D2, Obi Wan Kenobi and Luke Skywalker. I wish it
had Yoda. Yoda is my all-time favorite movie character.
The dogs are lying down on the floor next to me sleep-
ing. It's an early night for them. They must have played
hard today. I'm a little tired too. I cleaned house, sewed
costumes for the play and helped Andrea with her
computer... oh, and cooked dinner and baked a cake.
(No wonder I'm tired.) I'll write again tomorrow. Have
a good night. Pleasant dreams! Love, Mom

Once again, my writings to him were filled with everyday events.
He liked that. It took his mind off of his circumstances and into
another place. He would picture images in his head of the events I
shared with him. It helped keep him grounded and sane.

Remembering the Sheep

May 31, 2011 – In pencil, on letter size, yellow lined
note pad paper Joshua hand wrote to me:

Hi Mom,
I'm writing cuz there are a few things I would like to
reminisce with you about. Do you remember when we
used to live in Hemet? Well, I was reading a passage
from Matthew 25:32. It talks about how Jesus will come
back and shepherd his people. It made me think of all
the open fields in Hemet and how we always used to
see the shepherd with his flock and his lil' trailer, and
no matter what part of town or what road, he always
seemed to be in a field near to wherever we were. But
we would never see them in transit. Makes me wonder.

Makes me think of my relationship with God. No matter where I go or what road I'm on, He's always near, waiting for me to come join His flock. Hey Mom, maybe this "time" I've been given is a blessing in disguise.

The other memory is about the day, we lived in those apartments, when, (obviously I was doing something bad) you started to spank me. You were mad. I looked at you and kinda started to laugh. Then you started to laugh cuz you and I both knew that spanking me wouldn't work anymore. Then we both broke out into hysterical laughter. I think that was the day you became more than just my Mom. You became my friend. :)
Love you, Mom. Josh

Joshua was a very sweet child, yet a bit of a scamp. For example, the apartment we lived in when he was about 10 years old had a door knocker. When used, the pitch was very high and ear splitting. Every day when we got home, he would lift the door knocker and bang it back down. And every day, I would tell him not to, until one day, I finally had to take action to get him to listen. The story he told in the letter above was one of those moments. Joshua was talking back to me. I kept telling him to stop. He would laugh and keep it up. When I had finally had enough, I reached over to swat him. It was immediately obvious that he was too grown up for a swat from Mom to have any impact on him. We both ended up laughing so hard we could hardly catch our breath! When he wrote me about it, I knew right away what he was talking about. It seemed like such a small thing at the time! To Joshua, it was clearly much more.

Sharing the Journey

June 3, 2011 – Email to my Worship Pastor and Friend:

Hi Teresa,
I used to have this dream/vision... something... In it

Joshua would be sitting off stage while I spoke to a group of people. I would tell his story of addiction and jail. At the end of the message, I would introduce Joshua to the audience so they could see how God had transformed him. Now, maybe the dream isn't exactly how things will be, but I think God showed me that so I would know not to give up on Joshua--no matter what was said to me or to him. It has been a really long haul. Many people have said and done so many unkind things. What made it even harder was the fact that I could not explain to them what God had shown me. With Josh firmly in the midst of his difficulties, it would have sounded silly for me to speak about how he was going to be healed one day.

Many people don't understand addiction, or simply don't want it in their lives. They view it as a dead-end road, and fear the addict's lies, manipulation, stealing, and erratic behavior. I genuinely understand their point of view.

Recently, God has given me this scripture... "Mary kept these things and pondered them in her heart." I knew what it meant. She held a secret about her son, too. She had to wait for the right time. She knew he was different. She knew that if she told people about the real plan for him, they would laugh at her. After all, to them, he was only a poor Hebrew boy. He was probably barefoot and dirty most of the time. Now, I am not comparing myself to Mary, or comparing Josh to Jesus. I am putting forth that God used that story to speak to me about my son. Only a Mother would remember the specific details of her child's birth. Only a Mother would have the

eyes to see into her child's future and know that he was
meant for better things. Only a mother would have a
heart of sacrifice--enough to accept insult and mockery
just to be near her child. Only a son could bring such
pain and pride.

We will see what the future holds. We will see how the
next few years play out for Joshua. For me, God has
told me not to "speak to him like a child, but to speak
to the child within him," so healing may occur. That's
why I was so nervous to go visit him in jail last night.
I wanted to say the right thing. It was funny: Joshua
was the one who was saying all the right things, not me.
God has such a great sense of humor! Love, Gayle

Because of Joshua's long term addiction I have story after story of
God intervening in his life. Sadly, I also have story after story of terrible things being said to me about Joshua and my inability to parent
him. It seemed that in the most trying time of my life, no help could
be found. I tried to find counseling, work, help and support for him.
Options were limited. Free drug rehabilitation centers were few and
far between, and most were already full (Drug Abuse has become a
national affliction. Josh says that it was a pestilence of Biblical pro-
portions.) Even friends and family turned away. They were scared
that what I was facing would somehow spill over onto them. They
were scared Joshua had become someone other than himself and
would harm them. Some talked behind my back about how I had
ruined my child. I remember once, Joshua went to my Mom's house
to get something to eat, because he had been living in a drug house
where there was no food. My Mom was on vacation, but my niece
was staying there. Her step kids were there during the day while
she was at work. When she found out that Joshua was there, she
told them to get out of the house. She then called my mom on her
cell phone and told her that Joshua was breaking into her house

(though he had a key) and she was going to call the police. She was afraid of Josh. My Mom called me and told me to get Josh out of her house before the police showed up. I called my Mom's home phone and when the answering machine picked up, I said, "Joshua, if you are in Grandma's house, leave now. Your cousin is calling the police to have you arrested for breaking in." After I hung up, I called my niece. I tried to tell her that Joshua was probably hungry and tired and wanted to get something to eat and maybe a little rest. He wouldn't hurt her.

She wasn't having it. All I could do was hope that Joshua had heard the message I had left. Later Josh told me that he was standing in the kitchen with the fridge open looking for something to eat when he heard the phone ring. The answering machine picked up and he heard my voice. He said he couldn't believe what he was hearing. Later on when we talked about that day he said, "I guess you really do have eyes in the back of your head, Mom. You always seem to know what I'm doing." That was funny, but also sad.

Family members were frightened of him because of his behaviors and Joshua seemed hell bent on self destruction. All I could really do was pray. My influence over his actions was limited. I began to turn to God's word to learn about healing. I pressed into God; He was all I had. As it turns out, He was all I really needed. I worshipped, I fasted, and I prayed. I learned Biblical truths and began to apply them to my life, to Joshua's life, too. At times, I felt I would not survive. I thought that Joshua would not survive. I could not understand why we were going through such an awful time.

As it turns out, what was meant for harm, God used for good. I was changing. I was being healed. Who would have guessed that would be the outcome?

As the criticisms against me mounted and everyone had an opinion of what I should do and how I should do it, and as Joshua's behavior became more and more dangerous, I was forced to make some very radical choices. Do I listen to the world and turn away from my son? Or do I follow the promptings of the Holy Spirit and obey what I believed God was speaking into our situation? Do I turn my back on my boy because he wasn't acting in a way that made me proud, or do I throw my pride away and work at remaining in a relationship with him?

Ultimately, with my back against the wall, I chose to follow God and I chose to love Joshua. This was a life altering time for me. I had spent most of my life seeking approval. Now, I was in a situation that was asking the polar opposite of me. It was a lesson I desperately needed to learn. As I moved forward into this new point of view, I felt scared and unsure. I asked God to help me and God was faithful.

God Has a Plan

June 5, 2011 – After a (collect call) phone conversation with Joshua where he told me I was one of his best friends, I wrote him the following:

Dear Joshua,
Well, if I am one of your best friends, I take that as a compliment now that you're an adult. That was a very nice thing for you to say. Moms like to hear that kind of thing from their kids. Helps them - helps me - feel like the mistakes I made weren't so bad after all. We sure have been through a lot together. :) That's OK. I wish you didn't have to face this new circumstance. It stinks. I like the changes I see in you though. I feel like they are going to "stick" this time. God has a plan. I have always believed that. When everyone told me to give up on you, I believed God had a plan. When people wondered why I believed in you, it was because I knew God had a plan. I knew I shouldn't give up. If I did, who would tell you about God's plan?

I had to hang on. You needed to know. It was my job to tell you until you could hear God's voice for yourself.

In the passenger seat of the car, you were a captive audience. I quoted scripture, because I knew you would understand it someday. God's plan could not be accomplished unless you knew the difference between right and wrong. Sometimes people assume that because of your history, I would not feel close to you. That has never been the case. We have always stuck together. Our relationship never grew distant or cold. I think that's because of God's plan. He will never let you go. He will continue the good work in you until it is complete.

I am excited to see what the future holds for you. As long as you hold on to this newfound faith, the future holds good things. What will you do, where will you go and whose life will you impact? Will you carry Christ to the darkest of places? Will you counsel others who have faced your same issues? Will you live a simple life and share Christ in everyday locations? Or, maybe it's all of the above? Either way it works out, you will be much happier with Jesus than without, regardless of what you do.

(Pslams1:41)
God blesses those people who refuse evil advice and won't follow sinners or join in sneering at God. Instead, the Law of the Lord makes them happy, and they think about it day and night. They are like trees growing beside a stream, trees that produce fruit in season and always have leaves. Those people succeed in everything they do. That isn't true of those who are evil, because they are like straw blown by the wind. Sinners won't have an excuse on the day of judgment, and they won't have a place with the people of God. The LORD protects everyone who follows Him, but the wicked follow a road that leads to ruin.

*Here's proof for you. It's in the scriptures. And you
know you are such a sweet boy: sweet natured and kind
hearted. You have always been sweet and kind, even
while living dangerously, both when you were a child
and as a man. Your sweetness and kindness will take
you a long way. With God protecting and caring for
you, there is no worry of harm. We live in a lost and
dying world. We should reach out in love every chance
we get. That's not always easy, but when you think
about what's at stake, it seems a little less difficult. Go
forward with hope--without fear. After all, if God is
on your side, what does it matter who is against you?
Sleep tight. Pleasant dreams. Love, Mom*

I was doing my best to speak hope into Joshua's heart and mind.
I knew that if he felt hopeless, his time in custody would be much
more difficult to face. Even with hope, it was going to be a long,
hard haul. I wasn't sure if I was saying or doing the right things.
I only knew what the Bible says about the scriptures--they do not
return void. I felt that if I shared scriptures with him—even if they
weren't right for the moment--they would be right for some circumstance he may be facing in the future. It really was the very best that
I could do. God's word never fails.

God Will Make a Way

June 7, 2011

*Dear Josh,
I bought you more money, more phone time and more
food. You should have it shortly. I also checked on the
last order. I think I might have made a mistake, but am
waiting to hear back.*

*Keep reading the Bible. Also, develop a thankful heart.
Thank God for His love, even when you aren't feeling it.*

> *Being thankful will create a breakthrough. Praise Him,*
> *and He will shatter the chains in your heart and mind*
> *that hold you captive. I know, because I have done it*
> *myself. You're gonna be all right. God is on your side.*
> *He is making a way. Love, Mom*

It's not easy to maneuver through the jail system, especially if you're not used to it. You would think with all the time that Joshua had spent in jail (7 ½ years of the past 15), I would know how to get money to him, or schedule visits, but I still didn't have it perfected. This was another worry for me. If I sent him money, would he even get it? What if I did it wrong and it went to someone else? What if I told Joshua I was going to visit him and then made a mistake on the scheduling system and couldn't get in to see him? In addition to worrying about my son's physical, emotional and spiritual well being, there was the added layer of how the process worked: the rules and regulations of the county jail. Talk about stressful! I was in constant prayer things would work out.

I never told Joshua that I felt that way. One day, when we went to visit, my husband mentioned it. I immediately gave him a look of daggers coming from my eyes. That was supposed to be a secret! Upon learning about this, I saw Joshua look down and could tell a sadness had come over him. He now knew that his behavior and consequent circumstance were causing me pain. I had never shared that with him before. I had always tried to be strong. I think maybe it was a good thing for him to see my weakness and pain. Seeing my heart helped to change Joshua's heart. As always, God came through; He had given just the right thing at just the right time.

My husband and I, along with our pastor, had committed to praying for Joshua every day. It was especially meaningful to me that my pastor had taken an interest in standing beside us in our hope for Joshua's future. Very few people were willing to do that while Joshua was in the midst of his addiction. I felt blessed in knowing that there was someone, finally, willing to believe with me. It helped lift my head and lighten my load. And just between you and me, I don't think Joshua was the only one he was praying for; I think he might have been praying for me, too.

Heartbreaking Circumstances

June 12 , 2011 – My Pastor emailed me and asked me for Joshua's address in jail so he could write to him. My response:

Dear Pastor,
Sure. He has asked me several times if you are going to write to him. He seems eager to hear from you. He says things that make me hopeful. At first he was saying, "I give up." To me, that implies an exhaustion that does not necessarily carry a conscious choice. Now he is saying, "I surrender," which seems to me to be more of a decision. I know it's just verbiage, but for me, it has a different meaning.

I feel like God is telling me to handle things differently too. I am not sure everyone is going to understand that change. Once again, I am in the position of having to choose God's way to deal with my son. I have been harshly criticized in the past for listening to God. Everyone has an opinion. The thing is, I know Joshua really well (of course). I know how bad (wicked) he has been. I have walked away from him, not visited him, had him arrested and taken from my home in handcuffs. I have refused his calls, told him to leave my mother's home, things that it seems I should never have had to do: heartbreaking things. Through it all, I prayed and hoped.

It's a torturously thin line you walk when dealing with addiction. You never know when the moment is right to show grace, or the moment to show tough love. I prayed and I prayed and I prayed. For 15 years I have prayed. I have faced the fact that I may bury my son. I have

31

faced the fact that people have blamed and shunned me for Joshua's behavior. When it seems as if he is changing, I am afraid to hope. Yet I can't keep myself from hoping that somehow, someday, I will have my son back. It's like a flag being twisted in a driving wind. I am tattered and worse for the wear, yet still anchored to my standard. I just can't let go. I will not let go until there is proof that hope no longer exists.

Here is Joshua's address. Thank you for taking the time to write to him. Josh was raised in church and has had several close relationships with pastors. I think he secretly likes it. He will be sentenced this Thursday. They have talked about 16 months times 2 because he has prior DUI convictions. He is going to state prison. He is hoping to be sent to fire camp somewhere nearby, with credit for time served. That will mean approximately 2 years at the camp. I can go see him if he is placed locally. It would be great if you could pray for that to occur. After sentencing, he may be moved as quickly as the very next day. This address may only be good until then. Thanks, Gayle

The Wind is Blowing the Wrong Way

June 13, 2011

Hi Mom,
It was good seeing you and Grandma yesterday. Isn't Grams a cute old lady? Hey Mom, thanks for being here for me. Usually you would say, "You're on your own." However, I think that you see the honest sincerity in me when I say, "I'm done." So Mom, you know how I said that every time this happens (getting arrested) it always feels like a grey day. What I mean by a grey day

is nothing feels quite right. Like the wind is blowing the wrong way. Whatever road I'm on feels like a dead end. The songs on the radio aren't singing the right words. Everything just feels misaligned, or out of place. It's the same feeling every time. Except this time when I was driving along, I kept seeing groups of people enjoying themselves. One group was playing a softball game, and another was on the side of the street in a big circle holding hands and praying. As I passed these different groups, I couldn't help feeling all alone. At one point, I almost stopped the truck and went and joined them. It was almost as if God was speaking to me, saying to come join the flock of laughter and love and leave all the hurt and sorrow and loneliness of my sinful ways. You know Mom, there's a reason I didn't stop the truck. I wouldn't have got the fullness of God's lesson and the life that He's got planned for me! It's almost as if He was showing me where I belong. Love, Josh

P.S. Love you, Mom. You're great. Thanks for being there for me.

Joy! Reading Joshua's letters about how he was "done" and realizing that he was acknowledging God, brought joy. I found myself smiling inwardly even though I hadn't yet dared to admit to anyone else that this time things really did seem different, that Josh seemed different. Out of that joy poured my love for him.

I'm Always Here for You

June 15 , 2011

Hi Josh,
I wanted to write and say I love you. I love you no matter what. I think of you always. I wonder about your health and safety. I wish for your happiness. I pray for

*your salvation. Not a moment of my life goes by where
thoughts of you are not flooding my heart. Don't ever
forget that. I am always here for you. Love, Mom*

It's Nice to Have Him Back

*June 22, 2011 – After several visits and phone conver-
sations with Joshua, I wrote this email to my Pastor:*

*Hi Pastor,
I wanted to tell you the latest from Joshua. He said
he wants a new Bible. Once he gets to (hopefully) fire
camp, he asked me to go to the bookstore and buy a
Bible and have them ship it to him. I said I would. He
chuckled a bit and said that he has already worn out
the one he has in jail. He said, "I read it when I'm
awake, I sleep with it, and one day I woke up with it
stuck to my face." I thought that was pretty funny. He
said his Celly (that's what they call their cell mates)
can't tell if he is awake or asleep because even when he
is asleep he has his Bible open. Oh, Joshua... he could
always make me laugh. It's nice to have him back, even
if he isn't home. Thanks, Gayle*

Once Again, the Ordinary

June 24, 2011

*Hi Josh,
It was nice to see you yesterday. I forgot to tell you, Fino
vacuumed the inside of the Jeep engine with my house
vacuum cleaner. It was filled with black stuff. I told him
from now on he had to use the shop vac. He's such a dork
sometimes. Lauren* [my granddaughter] *is here today. We
are going to Target to get me some new sandals; I have*

*worn a hole through the sole of my old ones. Not sure I
like the new styles. They seem to highlight my fat toes.
I am doing an inventory of all the props and costumes I
have in my garage for the drama dept. That should keep
me busy for a while. Miss you. Love, Mom*

A Memory to Make Joshua Smile

June 26, 2011

*Hi Josh,
It's Sunday and I'm getting ready for church. I was
putting my eyeliner on and it reminded me of how you
described your friend putting on her make up with her
shaky hand. My biggest problem getting ready in the
morning is my eyebrows. I can never get them even. I
look like I'm perturbed all of the time. You know, with
one brow higher than the other. I'm going to sit down
today and write you a letter. I will be coming to visit
again as well. Till then, take care and I love you.
Love, Mom*

June 27, 2011

*Dear Joshua,
Well, here is the letter I promised. Sorry it took so
long. I feel like I always have something I'm supposed
to do... even though I'm not working. And speaking
of that, I have applied for more jobs than I can even
count. Sometimes as many as 7 in a week, with no response. It's crazy that I can't find a job. So I have been
stressing about finances. I think God wants me to learn
to let go of the things the world provides and trust Him*

to provide. I swear it's giving me ulcers! Sunday I sang for all 3 services. I went home and changed into more comfortable clothes and got back in time for the Span-ish services 1-year anniversary celebration. They had a mariachi singer and then a Spanish worship singer. She was like Pastor Teresa, but Hispanic. It was really good.

Then Raul (our friend who runs the Spanish services) gave the message. It was about this... "You have been faithful with a few things; I will put you in charge of many things." (Matthew 25:23) The sermon was "What do we do when God calls on us? Do you answer with excuses?"

Excuse #1 – Lack of Preparation: Moses said to God, "Who am I that I should go to Pharaoh and bring the Israelites out of Egypt?" *God said,* "I will be with you. And this will be the sign to you that it is I who have sent you." *(Exodus 3:11-12)*

Excuse#2 – Self Doubt: Moses said to God, "Suppose I go to the Israelites and say to them, 'The God of your fathers has sent me to you,' and they ask me, 'What is his name?' Then what shall I tell them?" *God said to Moses,* "I AM WHO I AM. This is what you are to say to the Israelites. I AM has sent me to you." *(Exodus 3: 13 14)*

Excuse #3 – Lack of Resources: Then the Lord said to him, "What is that in your hand?" "A staff," *he replied. The Lord said,* "Throw it on the ground." *Moses threw it on the ground and it became a snake and he ran from it. (Exodus 4:2-3)*

*God requires just one thing from us--Respond in faith.
God told Abraham,* "Leave your country, your family
and your father's home for a land that I will show you.
I'll make you a great nation and bless you. I'll make
you famous; you'll be a blessing." *(Genesis 12:1-2)*

*And all of this was in Spanish. I'm not saying God
worked a miracle and I could suddenly understand another language (the sermon notes were in English), but
I am saying that since I didn't seem to be listening to
God in English, he had to try something else to get my
attention. I guess I better stop doubting whether or not I
am good enough, or if people will listen, or how we are
going to make ends meet, to leave my comfort zone and
to respond in faith.*

*Also, I have included some pictures that I thought you
would like. I hope they give them to you. I am never
sure what gets through and what doesn't. Take Care.
Love, Mom*

જ‍જ

When Joshua was very young, he had a favorite green blanket that
he took everywhere with him. He called it "Greenie." He also had
a favorite stuffed rabbit. His Aunt Trina hand-made it for him as
a Christmas gift. He was and is very fond of her. True to form, he
named his treasured rabbit, "Rabbie."

Joshua's Carrot
He found it one night at chow (dinner). The inmates were given
baby carrots as part of their meal. You know the small peeled ones
that come in bags at the grocery store. Well, Joshua happened to
find one that still had a bit of green on top. He wondered, "Would
it grow?" He snuck it back to his cell. (Even carrots are considered

contraband; and therefore, not permitted in cells). Jail cells have a single window, which are rectangular in shape, about 3 feet long by 6 inches tall, with frosted glass preventing anyone from seeing in or out. Joshua was bold enough to ask the "Pill Lady" for one of the small plastic cups used to hand out medicine. He filled the small cup with water, put in the carrot, and placed it in the cell window. He said he wasn't sure if it would grow without dirt.

I have to tell you, this simple gesture of trying to bring life to such a desperate place deeply touched my heart. Then again, that was Joshua. No matter what his circumstance, he could or would bring something good. Remarkably, with only water and sunlight, the carrot started to grow. It got so big, it became the talk of the "tank" (the area of the jail where Joshua was being housed with approximately 30 inmates) and Joshua became somewhat of a carrot guru. Other inmates started bringing carrots back from chow, showing them to Joshua and asking him if they would grow (most of the inmates had come from such tough urban backgrounds they had never grown anything on their own). Sometimes, they would have a good one, with a little bit of green on it. Other times he would tell them, "No... that's not a good one. It's gotta have a little life left in it in for it to grow." His carrot, well, the leafy green top of it anyway, grew to be about 6 inches tall. Pretty impressive considering it had only light and water to sustain it. He would tell me about it in his letters and during phone conversations. It helped him keep his mind off of all the negative things that surrounded him.

I told one of our pastors at the church about Joshua's carrot. He used it as an analogy during one of his sermons. Josh too, used the carrot as a point of explaining new life and growth to fellow inmates. God was using this little carrot to teach us all a simple lesson about His love. With the sun, His son, shining down on us, and water, the living water of His Holy Spirit to sustain us, we can grow and thrive anywhere and in any environment. Here is a letter inspired by Joshua's carrot.

And by the way... he named the carrot "Carrie."

May You Always Have Dirt

June 28, 2011

Dear Joshua,
I loved your story about the carrot, about new growth.
It was really touching. It made me start to cry. I didn't
want to cry on the phone with you, but I just kept think-
ing about it after we hung up. I thought to myself, "He
didn't have dirt." It made me think of when you were
growing up and I couldn't afford to give you the same
things that other kids had. It was so strange, but I kept
thinking, "I wish he had dirt." Who would wish for
their child to have dirt, right? What I was really feeling
is that sense of going without. I never wanted you to go
without. I wanted you to have every good thing your
heart desired. Every chance, every joy, every blessing.
Yes, even dirt, so you could grow a carrot and see new
life. New life like the one that is growing within you.
The ground has been tilled, the soil fertilized, the seed
planted, and now, growth. May you always have dirt.
Love, Mom

On June 29, 2011 I wrote an email to my Pastor:

Hi Pastor,
Here is the latest on Joshua. He was having a really
hard time. He's so upset the he is losing 2 years of
his life, and tired of sitting in a jail cell. He had to go
back to court on July 15th for sentencing on his parole
violation. It should run concurrent to his sentence for

the DUI. He will go from there to George Bailey for a couple of weeks. It's a really rough place. Then he goes to Donovan State Prison. They lock the prisoners down for 23 hours a day. They are under investigation for civil rights violations. It's a bad place. If he can't get to fire camp, he will spend the next 2 years locked in a 4 by 4 cell. Horrible. Please pray for Fire Camp.

(I also shared Joshua's carrot story.)

Praying
for Fire Camp

Communication is a Two Way Street

July 3, 2011 – I hadn't received a letter from Joshua for a while, so in a phone conversation I teasingly told him I wouldn't write him anymore letters if he didn't write one back to me. Joshua heard me and wrote:

> *Dear Mom,*
> *So, I guess what you're saying is that correspondence is a two way thing... Hahahaha. Well, I suppose I'll keep up my end of the deal and send you this letter. However, the reason I don't write as much is probably cause there's not a whole lot of things going on around here worth writing about. It's pretty much like this... BLAH! It's like this: I wake up, eat, go to sleep, wake up, eat, go to sleep, wake up eat, take a shower, go to sleep. Shall I continue or do you get the point? When I usually write, (which isn't too often) it's when I have a breakthrough. That or when I'm struggling with some-thing and it inspires me to write. (That's usually the good stuff.) I think that listening and talking to God has softened the blow of the internal struggles. Anyways, I just got side tracked, lost my train of thought. Love you, Mom. Hope to hear from you soon. Love, Josh P.S. I read Proverbs 3:11 & 12 today. (It says, "My son, do not despise the LORD's discipline, and do not resent his rebuke, because the LORD disciplines those he loves, as a father the son he delights in.")*

July 5, 2011 - In phone conversations with Joshua, I began to notice changes in his tone and in his comments. It seemed God had taken Josh to the mountaintop, and now he was crashing back down. I was afraid that would happen. It's hard to stay up and excited when you're in jail. It just is. So with the story of his carrot fresh in my mind, I sent him this email:

> *Dear Josh,*
>
> *Here is a Bible lesson I found on living water: "Satu-rated But Not Strong." (John 7:37 – 39)* [In the Bible, Jesus is referred to as "living water."] *You know, maybe it's time for us to see that our roots need to be growing, not just our leaves. Do you know some things about the Lord that you didn't know a month ago? Have you given Him some new ground that he didn't have a month ago? Are you praying in fresh, new ways? Are you going by the book and not by your feelings? The Holy Spirit is often represented with the imagery of water, symbolizing His power to wash us clean of sin and nourish us spiri-tually. Jesus promises living water to all who sincerely ask for it. Don't let your newfound faith dry out and blow away like dust in the wind. Love, Mom*

The Crowd At The BBQ

> *July 6, 2011*
>
> *Hello Pastor,*
> *My last few conversations with Joshua are showing signs of my concerns being realized. He seems to be losing his initial fire for God. Part of that is because he is clean now. No drugs or alcohol in his system. He is on a more even course. When he was first arrested he was still under the influence and he was scared. He was*

reaching out for the hand of God to rescue him. When that didn't happen, he began to realize that he needed the presence of God to sustain him. Now he is wondering, "Is it real? Will it help?" The old mind-sets and thought processes are coming back into play. I wake up in the morning and pray for the Holy Spirit to fill him, mind and soul. I used the carrot as a lesson. (He said it is so big now that it has outgrown the cup.) I sent him the verses in John that talk about the streams of living water. It's relatable because the carrot is thriving on water alone.

I went to a BBQ on the 4th of July. As usual, it was mentioned that Joshua was the only one in the family that was "in jail." Instead of staying silent I decided to take a (gentle) stand. I talked about how God was redeeming Joshua, and how he was growing in Christ every day. I talked about his carrot, too. I knew that God could take the bad and use it for good. I preached to the crowd. I used Joshua's journey. I was not going to have Joshua or I held under the cursing words of mean spiritedness. We are all sinners, falling short of the glory of God. Joshua's sin just lands him in jail. I am no better than him and neither was the crowd at the BBQ.

I refuse to be labeled. I refuse to allow Joshua to be labeled. We are free in Christ! And besides, Joshua is mine. I love him and he loves me. We are very much in a relationship with one another… always have been. Isn't that what life is all about? Do I wish he made better choices? Of course. Still, as I said, he is mine and I am his. From conception into eternity that will be true. I wait and I pray. I live on the side of hope and not despair. I am a conqueror. I have learned that from

*Joshua and his struggles. In truth, I have learned more
from Joshua than I have from any other single person.
He is, was and will always be a gift. I love him just as I
love my daughter.*
Thank you for listening. Gayle

Got to Get to Fire Camp

July 7, 2011

Hi Josh,
*I finally talked Fino into getting an above ground pool.
Woohoo! Fino and I spent most of yesterday working
on the yard, cleaning it up and pulling weeds. I have a
thorn in my finger tip that I can't get out. Hurts every
time I bump it.*

*I am praying that you will go to a fire camp nearby
so that I can spend time with you. I want to make sure
you get your allotted dose of nagging! I am going to sit
down tonight and write you a letter. I love you.*
Love, Mom

*July 8th, 2011 – an email I wrote to my Pastor who had
been asking about Joshua's welfare.*

Hi Pastor,
*Joshua asked me to call his parole officer to find out if
his points are low enough for him to get into fire camp.
I don't really understand it all, but if they are too high,
he will have to stay in Donovan. I talked to the parole*

*officer today and he said he could not find any informa-
tion in Joshua's file and that it is usually something that
the prison system handles anyway. I emailed Josh to
give him the update. I told him that maybe God wanted
it that way, so we would rely on Him to change things
and not man. I told him that I think we should both pray
about it every day. I gave him a time of 9:30am which I
am going to try very hard to consistently do. I told him
that I would ask you and Fino to pray with us. Although
with your busy schedule, I know that 9:30am might not
work. The prayer time is mostly for me and Josh to feel
connected. I hope you don't mind.*

*We would like Josh to be somewhere close so that Fino
and I can go visit him, but if not, any fire camp is better
than Donovan State Prison. I wanted to update you on
the carrot too. The guys in jail are all interested and
fascinated with the carrot. They want him to leave it
there when he moves on, so it can remind them of the
Holy Spirit. Josh told them that he can't leave it behind,
that the Holy Spirit is something they need to carry
within themselves. Besides, he wants to eat it!
Thank you for the prayers. Gayle*

Finding Freedom

The Lord Helps Me Fly

July 11, 2011 – In pencil, on letter size, yellow lined note pad paper Joshua wrote to me:

Dear Mom,
I'm not sure what to do here. I wish I could explain to you in detail what really goes on in here, but I can't. Even if I could, I'm not sure I'd want to. What I will say is that it's like dealing with a bunch of six year olds or worse, a bunch of men that grew old, not up.

Mom, you know I was thinking about what I said to you earlier about how I said it's other people's actions and not mine. Well I was wrong. It was my actions that got me in this mess! However, the realization of that still doesn't change how others act, only how I act. I just hope and pray that they come to the same conclusion. OK, so that was yesterday's news. You know, I think that's part of the problem. People are always living in the past instead of living in the present day and trying to make the future better.

So, now I'm on a whole other day. Today went very well. I went to the yard all by myself. Everyone else was asleep. It was great. It was a cool, crisp morning with a little breeze. At first the marine layer was blocking out the sun, but as I was walking and thinking and enjoying,

*the clouds started lazily drifting on with the wind. It
was calm, quiet, peaceful and warming as the morning sun was waking. I sat down in the shade and talked
with God as the breeze danced across my shoulders. It
was 9:30am and pleasant. I only hope yours was just as
enjoyable. Mom, its kinda funny, cuz I didn't realize the
time until I returned to my cell. Also, I found a positive
solution to a negative problem. Mom, you're awesome.
I'm glad that we have this special friendship.
Love, Josh*

*P.S. I wrote a lil poem with this letter.
Patiently waiting for the day I can fly
They keep me locked in a cell, Lord only knows why
They try to suppress me, n' keep me from flight
It's only a moment, a lapsing in time
Someday they'll release me to play in the sky
They cannot contain me for my wings they are wide
I will soar with the angels and God in the sky
They cannot contain me, the Lord helps me fly*

৵ৎ

July 13, 2011

*Dear Pastor,
Joshua called me this afternoon. He said he was feeling
better about things after several days of being really
stressed over his future and where he may end up. It's
challenging when you no longer have control over
where you spend your time and who you spend it with.
He said he got out to the "yard" today. It was morning and since he is in Vista (California), it was a bit
overcast. He said it was cool and relaxing. No one was*

in the yard with him. He tried to run some laps but it was too hard in his jail issue sandals. So instead, he sat down and started to pray. He was there for a while when he realized he needed to go back inside. When he got to his cell, he looked at the clock and discovered that he had been praying at 9:30am, the time that we have set aside to pray together. He said, "Mom, I was praying at the right time without even realizing it!" It made me stop and think about how God orchestrates even the smallest details of our lives, just so he can be close to us. The chances of Josh getting to the yard are slim. The chances of him being there alone are even slimmer. Yet on a cool morning, beneath a canopy of soft clouds, God met my son and they had a conversation. It makes me think of Jesus in the garden. What a beautiful picture that paints.

The same God that met Christ in the quiet moments before the crucifixion met Joshua in a prison yard. Freedom. Though he is locked up, Joshua is becoming free. Gayle

The Sentencing

July 15, 2011 – an email I sent to two of my Pastors:

Hi,
Joshua has court today at 1:30pm. They will get to him in whatever order he is on the docket. Please be in prayer. I want him to be placed where it will do the most good and the least harm. Only God has that answer. Thanks, Gayle

I was there that day. I watched them bring my son in wearing handcuffs and shackles. When he saw me he smiled. I smiled back, but in truth, my heart was breaking. As we waited to hear the news, I prayed. And then it came--2 years. That's a long time for a DUI, but not for repetitive DUIs. I kept thinking, "What if he had been drinking and driving and hit someone? How do you live with yourself after that?"

The Judge sentenced him to fire camp. It seems there is a process for everything in life and prison is no different. First, he would be moved to George Bailey Detention Facility and from there to Donovan State Prison and then finally, on to fire camp. The prison had the final say about whether or not Josh got fire camp, so it was still a prayer away.

For the first few months in Donovan, I was not able to speak to him. That was about 120 days. We would have to correspond through letters alone. No visits or phone calls were allowed. We were praying that things would move quickly for Joshua and that God would place him in a fire camp close enough for us to be able to visit. The last time he was sent away he was in Northern California, 8 hours away. I didn't see him for an entire year.

His time in George Bailey and Donovan definitely *did not* go quickly. But as always, God had a plan.

July 16, 2011

Hi Pastor,
Joshua wrote a poem about the morning he spent in
the yard by himself praying. He writes well. He always
has. My ex-husband used to spit the words at me ac-
cusingly, saying about Joshua, "He acts just like you."
Sometimes, I would get really mad and say back to him,
"Funny how that works. He has my DNA and I raised

him. Shocking that he acts like me." It wasn't nice, but I would get so annoyed that, after awhile, I just couldn't help myself. Anyway, he really is like me.

Your wife spoke the kindest words to me one day. She said, "God gave him you for a mother because He knew he would have struggles." It was just about the only positive thing I have ever heard regarding my parenting of my son. Everyone judges - even when they try not to. The bend always leans towards my inability to properly parent him. I am more used to it now. At first it hurt me badly. I still carry a constant ache inside of me. But, I still have a relationship with my son. That's what is most important, not my foolish pride. And, it is pride. I want people to see Joshua the way I see him--to see the talent. To see how much he loves his family. I just have to wait for God to get through to Joshua, and for Joshua to begin walking the path that God has chosen for him. Then God will allow people to see and appreciate him.

I am going to miss service this Sunday to go and see him for the last time before they move him to George Bailey, down in San Diego. From there, he goes to Donovan State Prison. The judge recommended fire camp, but even so, the prison has the final say. From the time he gets to Bailey and for the first months in Donovan, I will not be able to speak to him (probably 3 months). Hopefully, when I do hear from him, he will be in fire camp. Pray for a speedy processing to fire camp. Gayle.

July 16, 2011

Hi Josh,
Good news! I am scheduled to visit on Sunday. I feel
very relieved. I hope you have a great day today! Oh, I
loved the poem. It really expressed how it feels to be in
your situation. We'll get through this. Love, Mom

I never liked going to visit Joshua in county jail. First, there was the anxiety that something would go wrong and I wouldn't get to see him, and second, was the grunge and filth of being in the run-down county facility. It was just so gross! The rooms smelled bad and everything was covered with dirty fingerprints. The air was stale and artificial light masked the time of day. The poor lighting created a sense of claustrophobia.

We had to sign in an hour ahead of time and then wait for our time slot. Then, we showed our I.D. to go through the door that led to where the inmates are housed. There are arrows with section names painted on the walls so you know which corridor to take. The air is all recycled and there are no windows. It feels and smells like you have entered the bowels of hell. Once you get into the area where the phones are located, you pick a stool and sit down. They call your inmate and you wait for them to come through the door where they sit on stools on their side of the glass.

I would always feel nervous and uncomfortable in the narrow, concrete, windowless hallways until I saw Joshua. He always smiled when he came through the door and saw me. Suddenly all my anxiety would dissolve. Smiling back at him, we would both pick up our phones and start talking. Over a period of 15 years, I visited Joshua this way - off and on - when he was incarcerated. It wasn't easy, but I did it. Love is strong that way. I always tried to talk to him about God. It was the only hope I knew. If I could help Joshua find hope, I knew he could survive, and maybe one day, change.

The Job Interview and Other Miscellaneous Events

As if things weren't bad enough during this time, I also became unemployed. I had been working in lending and was let go around the time when the economy crashed and many home mortgages defaulted. After being laid-off, I couldn't find work anywhere, not in lending nor in any field, for that matter. Shortly thereafter, my husband was let go in a nationwide, 700-employee lay-off. Sometimes when it rains, it rains really hard.

We ended up having to move in with my Mom. My husband did a few remodeling jobs on her house in lieu of rent. It was a little crowded, but we made it work. We were there for 8 months before I finally landed another job, although not a great one. You know how they always say that if you don't have a job, it's hard to find one, but if you already have a job, you can always find another? Well, that definitely rang true for me. For two and a half years I couldn't find work. Within 6 weeks of finding one job, I was offered two more. These were both in my field. I took the one that paid the most and had the best benefits, and we were back in the game again. We rented a house that was only a 30-minute drive from where Joshua would eventually spend the bulk of his sentence. It made it much less stressful to go and visit him. My husband was eventually offered a position to join the staff at our church, which he accepted. If we could just get Joshua home, all would be well.

July 17, 2011

Hi Josh,
It was good to see you yesterday. I was really relieved
to get in. I thought for sure something was going to go
wrong. Please try to keep me posted on where you are.
I worry, you know. :) I am not sure if we can come on
Thursday due to finances being tight. I applied for a job
at a veterinary hospital. Could be fun. Don't overeat
and take care of the carrot. I love you. Love, Mom

July 21, 2011

Dear Joshua,

It's been an interesting week. Bet you wish you could say the same. Probably not much going on for you, huh? Well, Drea's [my close friend] *son Daniel spent the night. He's really cute! I have a job interview coming up, and a meeting for the kid's TV show I might be helping with. Fino put new tile down in the bathroom. It looks fantastic! It's almost a hundred degrees here and we can't afford to run the air conditioner! Other than that, things are good. Nick* [Josh's step brother] *got your letter. Never said anything about it though. He is a private guy, so I never expect him to share too much. I have had a terrible headache for about 3 days now. Not sure what that's about. It seems to coincide with my hot flashes. It's gnarly. My head hurts so bad that I am having trouble writing this letter. I took some Advil, but that only lasts for a while. Wah, wah! Speaking of health issues, how is the red spot on your hand? Did you go to the doctor yet?*

The interview process at the veterinary hospital went like this: I filled out the online application and was called in for an interview. I went in for the first interview and passed that. Now, I have to go to their office and work for 2 hours to see if I am a good fit. All the girls there wear scrubs, but I don't have any, so I asked what I should wear. The manager said to dress professionally. I have to wear my banking clothes cuz that's all I have! I hope I don't look too stupid being at a vet's office wearing high heels!!! Ugh! Why is my life always so weird?

You know how Chase [our dog] always attacks the sprinklers. They make him go crazy. He slept outside last night because Daniel was here and when they went off this morning, Fino had to rush outside and bring him in so he wouldn't chew the sprinklers up. Then, later today, after I put him outside, the neighbor behind us turned their sprinklers on. Chase stood at the fence looking longingly at them. When I take him on walks, if we pass a house with the sprinklers on, he lunges toward them. I think he is obsessed, or something. He's a weird dog.

I am waiting for the mail to see if my unemployment check comes. It's so much easier to work. Waiting to find out if they are going to hold my check or send it out is really stressful, especially when there are bills to pay. I guess we are OK. The bills are caught up (for now), we have food in the cupboards and we still have toilet paper, so I guess it could be a lot worse.

I hope you're doing OK. I hope Carrie (the carrot) is helping you maintain a good attitude even though you are in a somewhat negative environment. Just think of Paul and Silas and how, despite being in jail, they were filled with joy. I know... probably easier said than done. If there is a will there is a way.

I need to go now. I have chores to do and need to get ready for my "working interview" today. I'll let you know how it turns out! Hang in there Kemosabi.
Love, Mom

And then they moved my boy and my heart broke a little. I knew that I would have to go several months without speaking to him or seeing him. Right now, I really wanted to see him and speak to him. I was afraid.

My Turn to Reminisce

July 25, 2011

Dear Pastor,

They moved Joshua to George Bailey Detention Facility today. It's way down by the border. He tried to call me this morning but my phone was on vibrating mode and I missed his call. I am sure he is worried that I won't know where he is. I prayed that God would speak to his heart and let him know that I checked the Sheriff's website to see whether or not they had moved him. When I see his name and birthday on the screen, I remember back to the day he was born. That's when it gets me. It's when I feel the most pain. I see the name I chose for him, "Joshua Paul." I see his birth date and I think, "It started out so beautifully; how did it come to this?"

He was such a sweet little kid. He was a good student. He was tested for the gifted classes at school, but when I talked to him about moving to the classes for gifted students he said, "Mom, the kids in the gifted classes have to do so much more homework. I just want to be a normal kid. I go to school, and then I come home and play with my friends. I'm happy. I don't want to be in the gifted classes." I let the school know that Joshua would not be moving in the gifted classes. He was

*balanced and well. He started to change in 8th grade. I
am not really sure why. I asked him about it a few weeks
ago. He didn't answer me. Maybe he doesn't know why.
Maybe it still hurts too much to talk about.*

*I talked to him on the phone last night. I told him what
you said about God loving me and my boy so much
that he changed the entire prison system to make sure
he got to fire camp. He said it was hard to believe that
God would do that just for him. When I asked him if
it was because he didn't feel like he was worth it, he
went silent. Sometimes what people don't say speaks
louder than what they do say. Anyway, Josh is on the
move. First to George Bailey Detention Facility, then to
Donovan State Prison.*

*It is hard to accept, because he has violated the law and
lost his rights, my rights as his mother have also been
lost. I can no longer choose whether or not I can see or
hold my child. If not for the promise of God to care for
him, I would be thrown into complete despair. But I do
have God's promise for Joshua's best. Joshua accepted
Christ as a child, then in high school, and just after his
troubles began, he accepted Christ again. The youth
pastor who walked Joshua through the sinner's prayer
said that Josh broke down sobbing.*

*But after that, Josh stole a car, started running away
and began using drugs. During this time, he went to a
Christian sponsored New Year's Eve event. He was running on an inflatable obstacle course racing a friend.
He landed wrong and heard, "snap, snap, snap." He
had broken 3 bones in his foot. His friends dropped*

him off in our front yard. He hopped to the front door and knocked. I heard the knocking and got out of bed. When I opened the door Joshua hopped in and said, "I broke my foot." I asked, "Are you sure?" He said he was sure. I got dressed and took him to the Emergency Room. (Just in case you were wondering, never go to the hospital ER on New Year's Eve). They were so crowded that they didn't have any rooms available so they placed Joshua on a gurney in the hallway. We both fell asleep, him lying down and me sitting at the foot of the gurney with my head resting on it. We were there all night. Finally an orderly came and cut Joshua's (rather expensive) shoe off and took him to x-ray. He said it was really painful. They brought him out with a "foot boot" and said he needed to have surgery to repair the breaks; his foot was too swollen to do anything until a few days out. They gave us pain meds and sent us home.

A few days later, Joshua had surgery to have steel rods put in his foot so that the bones could heal properly. He was on crutches for 4 weeks and in a walking cast for another 2 weeks. The youth pastor I mentioned earlier told him the story of how the shepherd would break the leg of the sheep to keep them from wondering off into danger. Joshua's face went white and his eyes opened wide. I guess once again, he couldn't believe that God would care so much for him, enough to break his "leg" to save his soul.

Over the years, God has intervened in Joshua's life in remarkable ways. He knows God. He hears God. I don't know why he rebels against God. One night, in a drunken stupor, Joshua growled at me, "Why won't God

*just leave me alone?" Afterward, I wrote this and when
Joshua sobered up, I gave it to him.*

*"I once knew a young man who was living his life in
direct defiance to God. The louder God called his name,
the harder he rebelled until one day he said, "Why
won't God just leave me alone?" The voice that he
heard was human, but the response came straight from
the heart of God and it said, "Alone means by yourself,
with nobody else around. You're right. God won't leave
you alone." Jesus was a real man. He walked this earth.
They crucified him, but he rose again. He conquered
death to give us life.*

*After He rose again, before He returned to heaven,
He promised to come back for us. Until that time, He
left behind the beautiful remnant of his love and the
sweet perfume of his Holy Spirit because, after all, God
wouldn't leave you alone."*

*Joshua has caused me to re-evaluate my life. His pain
has allowed God to break my unbending spirit and drive
me to my knees in humility and submission. If not for
Joshua and the lessons I have learned from loving him,
I don't know where I would be. He has made my life
better on every level. First by being born, then by being
lost, and now, by being saved. Over and over again,
God has saved him. From drugs, from bad guys, from
self destruction, from the darkness. My prayer is that
the lessons God has taught me during these struggles
won't be lost on Joshua, and someday, he will be well
again and his story will help to heal many others with
broken hearts. What man plans for harm, God uses for
good. Love, Gayle*

*July 25, 2011 – an email I sent to Joshua in his new
location with the county:*

Hi Josh,
*Well, I hope your new home is OK. I wanted to send you
an email this morning, but the system wouldn't let me.
I just wanted to say I miss you and I have enjoyed your
carrot stories. I have shared them with lots of people.
Everyone keeps saying, "That's a screenplay idea."
Whatever. Anyway, I love you and I'll talk to you soon.
Love, Mom*

I Love Them All

July 26, 2011

Dear Mom,
*I'm not sure why God has us go through so many
struggles in life. It's very confusing. However, I find
that even in this evil, festering, dark, dark, miserable
place I can still find rays of "hopelight," whether it be
in God's word, prayer or sometimes simple things like
a bird flying or a smile on someone's face, the sound of
laughter or how God is working through me. I still have
bad days, but I know in my heart that I'm God's child
(He told me so) and that no matter what, I will be OK,
no matter where I am. I hope I can see you before I go
to state. I can't wait to get there and get through recep-
tion (the waiting period while they are processing your
paperwork to send you to a permanent location) and
then on to Jamestown (a prison fire camp in Northern
California). I know I will go. God wants me to. Mom I
will be sending a card to Liz* [his sister] *soon so give it*

> *to her, K? Tell everyone that I'm all right and that I love*
> *them all. Mom, I'm really glad that you're there for me.*
> *I love you lots. Write back soon. Love, Josh.*
> *P.S. You're awesome.*

And then there was silence for six days. I didn't hear from Josh again until August 1, 2011. He was being processed and there was no way for me to get in touch with him, or for him to contact me.

Happy, Joyful and Full of Life

> *August 1, 2011*

> *Dear Mom,*
> *I got shipped to state today. Sucks that I didn't get to see*
> *you and Grams one last time before I left. I'm going to*
> *send you a visiting form for Robert J. Donovan Deten-*
> *tion Facility, the place I'm at now. This facility is in the*
> *same valley as George Bailey is so it's not like you have*
> *to drive any further. When you get the form, fill it out as*
> *soon as you get it and include Grandma OK? The same*
> *day you get it, fill it out send it back, OK? Then after*
> *that, wait about a week and a half and call the prison to*
> *book a visit. It could be the last time I see you two for a*
> *long time. The reason you need to call and ask the jail*
> *if you're approved is cause by the time I get it, it will*
> *almost likely be too late. Another thing is tell Grams*
> *to try and get a hold of the money she put on my books*
> *before I left the county jail. They should refund her the*
> *$40.00 bucks. Also, try and call everyone and give them*
> *my new, temporary address, OK?*

> *Hey Mom, can you do me a favor and try to write and*
> *send me a letter every day? Plus tell Grams to send*

some stamps and envelopes in a manila folder. I also will try to write to you every day. Some more pictures would be nice to have. Or some of your stories that you like to write. Mom, I will write again tomorrow and try to think of anything else I've forgotten, K.

Mom, I really need you to help me get through this again. What I really need is God's help but it's hard to walk this fine line in here. On one side, I have to be tough and mean and scary and on the other side, I hope and dream and truly desire to be happy, joyful, and full of love and laughter. You know, to just smile and be content. That's not held in high regard in here. You know, I just want the comfort of the Lord with me always.

I sure do miss you, Lady. I really want to pour out the pain of what I have to go through, but I think I will save that for another letter, OK? I hope to hear from you soon. I will write again tomorrow.
Love, Joshua

P.S. Don't forget to let everyone know the address and send pictures
P.S.S. Mom, you must mail the visit forms. Address them to "visiting" I think, but just call or go online and find out. I'm not sure, so find out.

(When Joshua came home 2 years later, he indeed had become that happy, joyful, full of love guy that he hoped and prayed he would be. But, let's get back to the present time. Joshua had many more struggles to go through before he reached that goal.)

August 8, 2011

Dear Mom,
How's life treating you on your side of the razor wire? I
hope that all is well. Hey, any luck on finding a job yet?
Maybe you could get a job as a nurse in prison. Mom,
I remember why I keep drinking. It's because this place
is so awesome! LOL! Just kidding. Did you understand
the whole thing about sending a letter and sending the
visit form? It's the address or P.O box. Don't forget to
call about a week after you send it and schedule a visit.
Don't forget to send me some stamps and envelopes.
Did Liz get my card on time? Seems like a lot of ques-
tions, huh? Oh, can Grams write me and let know when
my clothes get to her house? It should be my shoes and
my new Levi's and boxers, although the list doesn't say
shoes. Did you already get those from county? Anyway,
let me know. Love you lots. Hope to hear from you soon.
Love, Josh

August 8, 2011 - that same day Joshua wrote another
letter to me:

Hi Mom,
I went to medical today. I had to put in a slip cause I
have ring worm on my chest and my lips are all dried
out and splitting. So, they gave me some stuff for that.
They charged me $5.00 and I found out they're taking
55% minus $5.00 bucks, so if you can J-pay me I'd like
another $50.00 bucks. That would be cool. Go online to
do it. Anyway, I also found out that it's taking us about
90 days to get out of here, unless God has other plans
for me :) However, I will send you some more visiting

forms, so you can give one to Fino. Mom, I haven't got any mail from you or anyone yet. What's up? Also, I'm running out of stamped envelopes, yo! I usually don't talk about it and I'm sure you don't want to hear about it, but try to imagine being locked in a cell for 23 hours a day with some guy who you've never met, only come out every three days for a shower (we get no deodorant so our pits smell like onions) and my stomach only stops growling for about 2 hours a day. But, I'm not complaining. Actually, I'm learning humility and just giving you a taste of what it's like here. I love you, Mom, and miss you. I can't wait to get some mail. Love, Josh

When I read back over the letters Joshua wrote to me, I feel the same sense of desperation from him that I did the first time I read them. Lots of worry (which is not like Joshua at all): Worry that he wouldn't get shipped out to Jamestown (the last fire camp he went to), worry that he wouldn't get his clothes back (the ones he was wearing the night he was arrested), worry that his sister didn't get her birthday card on time, worry that his Grandma wouldn't get her money back from the county jail... worry, worry, worry! It hurt me to know that my son was in such a place of despair. Still, I knew that God was in control and that there was a purpose to all of this.

About 12 or so years earlier, God had given me a vision of Joshua standing strong and tall. He was smiling and his eyes were filled with joy and light. We were in what looked like an airport boarding area. The walls were painted grey and it had rows of seats and unfamiliar faces. Joshua would enter through a door (it looked like a boarding gate to me) at the end of the room. Upon seeing me, he would smile a big, broad smile. Even though it didn't really make sense given the current circumstance and Joshua's fears, I held tight to that vision, believing that God would do as he promised. He would heal my son and make him strong and happy. What other choice did I have? To give up? I just couldn't. My heart wouldn't let me.

Louie Caught a Rat!

August 9, 2011

Dear Joshua,
Grandma got her money back. Don't worry about that
anymore. I got the visitations forms. I will send them
out today. I just got them on Saturday in the mail. Today
is the first available day to mail them back out. Things
are fine with everyone. Money is a little tight, but we
are working on fixing that. I am going to start selling
housewares. Linda (my childhood friend) is helping me.
I can't find a job anywhere else and besides, I'm not
sure I want to go back to the 8 to 5 thing. I might be too
old for it now.

Did you know that Louie caught a rat in the backyard?
It was 6 inches long, not including the tail. Here's what
happened... I was out in the backyard at Grandma's
house. I saw something on the fence top between
Grandma's house and the neighbor's house. The thing
dropped to the ground. Out of the corner of my eye, I
saw Louie. He moved like a bolt of lightning! WHAM!
He had the rat in his mouth. He caught it while it was
on the ground running. I had to pull him away from it.
He was trying to kill it even though it was already dead!
Grandma came out and while I held on to Louie, she
picked the rat up with a shovel and threw it in the trash.

I tried to pick it up, but it was too gross! I couldn't do it.
Grams was laughing at me. To get her back I told her
that she had to sleep with "Rat Breath" Louie. That's
his new nickname. I call him "Rat Breath." We took a
picture of the rat so we can show it to you. Anyway, I

hope you are doing OK. I hope the good news (about Louie catching a rat) enclosed in this letter cheers you up. Take Care! Love, Mom

Once again, I was telling him stories about ordinary stuff that was going on at home. To him, it was life giving, life affirming, especially the stories about his dog, Louie. :)

The Scent of Home

August 10, 2011 - Half man/half dog... Joshua has a really good sense of smell!

Hi Mom,
I just got my first piece of mail today. It's from you. The one with Louie's rat and Chapter One of your story. It was the strangest thing. Have you ever heard that your sense of smell is the best sense to trigger your memory? Well, I was taking a bird bath (out of the sink) when the cop banged on my door and slid a piece of mail through. I was all wet so I just slid the letter onto the table. (The mail in here has a certain smell). Weird, huh? I know. Well I was drying off and I caught a whiff of it, I instantly recognized the smell. I couldn't think from where, but I knew it was good. I think because we all so eagerly wait to hear from the outside world, and when we do, it takes us out of here if only for a moment.

I'm glad to hear that Grams got refunded her money. I loved the story about Louie and his "Rat Breath." LOL Hopefully the job selling housewares works out for you. I can hardly wait to read the next chapter in your book that you're writing. I like it a lot. Hope to hear and see you soon. Love, Josh

What I never told him about the chapter of the book I sent him was that he was the lead character. It's a story of a man who chooses with his heart and finds joy even in unpleasant circumstances. That sums up Joshua really well.

And then, out of the blue, Joshua wrote a letter to Fino. I don't really know what motivated it. Maybe Joshua felt like he was leaving Fino out of things by mostly corresponding with me. Fino had always been a part of our lives. He was almost an uncle to my kids as they were growing up. Whatever his reasons, it was a very touching letter, filled with evidence of God.

August 12, 2011

Fino,

It's kinda crazy the way that God works in my life. He sends me to the biggest, baddest places to do His work. He makes me strong when I am weak. When I don't know the words to be spoken, he guides my speech with words of wisdom and truth. He sends his love through me, to steer my neighbor from troubles. I walk through the valley of the shadow of death. I will fear no evil for His light guides my path. The path that He has set before me.

I have to admit even though the road is rocky it sure feels good to me. I know now that he's been running my whole life, molding and shaping me in my own special way that he sees fit, so I can spread His word and testament. You know, It's funny, no matter how hard I tried to do things my way and thought I knew what was best for me, I was wrong. I realize now that all the things my heart has truly desired can only be obtained through Him. I can honestly say that I'm ready for whatever He has in store. Love, Josh

He Dreamed He Ate a Giant Marshmallow

August 12, 2011

Dear Joshua,
I got your letter today. Sorry you haven't received my
letters yet, because the prison in-coming mail system is
slow. I don't really want to imagine what it's like for you
to be in prison. It turns my stomach. I sent the visita-
tion forms back, mine and Grandma's. I will send one
to Fino, too. You know what Nick [Josh's step brother]
told Fino the other day? Well, first of all, a while back
he told Fino that his moods go up and down. Then, just
before he moved out, he said he had a dream about a
"demon-looking thing" pulling him by the ankle. Every
time he would try to get up, it would pull him down
again. He said he woke up the next morning and his
ankle was sore. Fino said, "I know that you don't be-
lieve the same way Gayle and I do, but it's real Nick."
(He meant heaven and hell and angels and demons are
real.)

I was sort of creeped out thinking that there was a de-
mon in our house, then I got ticked off and decided that
the devil had no business in our house, messing with
our kids. It reminded me of the story about the guy who
dreamed he ate a 20 pound marshmallow. He woke up
the next morning and his pillow was gone!
Fino and I joined a co-ed softball team. I know, I know,
my glory days are over, but I still have fun playing. I
was way better than the other girls that showed up for
practice. One of them tried to catch a fly ball. It tipped
off of the top of her glove and hit her in the face. She
had to go to Urgent Care. It was pretty gnarly! I felt

*bad for her, but wondered why the guy hitting the balls
was hitting them so hard to her. She obviously wasn't
that skilled. It was like an accident looking for a place
to happen. She will probably never learn to play as
she will be ball shy. Oh well. Fino did pretty well. He
practiced batting left and right-handed and did really
well in the outfield. He always plays there because he is
so fast. Not bad for 51!*

*I miss you. Sometimes, I think of something funny you
said or did. It makes me sad. Then I realize that you're
still alive and that you're coming home one day. That
cheers me up. Or at least it helps. We all just have to
hang on until you come home. One day at a time, so to
speak. I am sure it's worse for you than it is for me. I
have things to do and places to go that help distract me.
You, not so much. Take Care, Josh. Love, Mom*

No More Squash

August 13, 2011

Dear Joshua,
*I got your letter today saying that you finally got a let-
ter from me. You should have gotten one from Grandma
too. Isn't it funny that you recognized the smell of
home? You really are part man, part dog. You have a
dog's sense of smell. I guess it could be worse. Dogs
are really good company! Well, at least some dogs are.
Anyway, I'm cleaning out the bedroom that Nick lived
in and getting ready to paint it. I bought a picture and
some new bedding. It seems dumb to have so many bed-*

rooms now. Fino and I live in our room and the living room. We never go into the other rooms. Oh well. I am filling out Fino's visitation form and sending it in. If he can get a day off, he can come. I'll have to check on the scheduling.

It's almost our 2nd anniversary. It's Aug 22nd. I think we are using our extra money to buy a wooden fence for our garden instead of going somewhere. Not sure. Fino wants to go to the beach and spend the night in a hotel or something. I guess that would be OK. I'd rather have a fence for the garden. We have cantaloupe and pumpkins, a ton of yellow squash and tomatoes, and some chive and sunflowers taller than the block wall fence. It's awesome. I want to start earlier next year and plant more stuff. No more squash, though. That stuff grows like crazy. We couldn't even eat it all. I had to start hiding it in stuff that I was cooking because Fino won't eat it otherwise. Chase sneaks into the garden every once in a while and stomps on all of our stuff. He learned that from Louie. Bad dog.

My Jeep is paid off now. No more payments! Not having to pay that anymore sure helps our finances. I need to pay our wedding rings off and then we should be sitting pretty. Then, if I can earn some money with selling housewares, things should be OK.

I will write another chapter of my story and send it out next week. Until then, remember that we haven't forgotten you. You're our Bubba J. - our Jodawa Paul. How could we forget? Besides, even if we do forget, the smell will help us remember! Love, Mom

The Scent of Home - Reprise
August 15, 2011

Hi Pastor,
I need to start from the beginning. Have you ever seen the movie "Space Balls?" It's a parody of Star Wars. In it, John Candy plays a character named Barf. He's part man, part dog. He says, "I'm half man, half dog. I'm a mog." Well, Joshua is really good with animals, dogs in particular. Even if your pet loves you, it will run to Joshua when he calls. So I always tell him, "You must be part man, part dog. You're a mog." Seriously, he does have a gift. Dogs just love him and vice versa.
[I then relayed the letter from Joshua about recognizing the scent of home. I finished the email by writing the following.] He recognized the scent of home, of me. I didn't spray perfume on it or anything. Just my handling it was enough. It cracked me up. I wrote him back and said that he really must be a mog! He even has a heightened sense of smell. Isn't that interesting? It was astounding to me that he recognized the scent. It made me laugh. I swear, I learn more from Joshua and his experiences then just about anything else in my life. Gayle

More Ordinary Things
August 17, 2011

Hi Josh,
It's me again. Just sending you a letter to keep you updated on the latest happenings. We have our first co-ed softball game tonight. I've never played on the same team with Fino. Should be fun. Then tomorrow, I have my first housewares show. I'm a little nervous, but

thankfully, it's at Christina's house [my niece] *so that should help a little. I think Christopher* [her little boy] *is going to be there. Maybe I can get him to help me. I think we are going to stay at a retro surf hotel in San Clemente for our anniversary night and spend the next day at the beach. Not sure. The hotel is an old motor inn. It has all these separate little rooms with their own parking spots out front. You walk to the beach. We sure could use a break. Things have been a little hectic around the homestead lately. That's OK. We're getting through it.*

Fino built a fence for my garden. He found some pallets that were being thrown away, took them apart and made a fence. They had 4X4 posts for the gate posts and slats for the fence, plus some 2X4s to use as the fence posts. It was perfect. I painted Nick's old room. It looks nice. I used light sage green, grays, black and white. It's very peaceful.

Chase is getting real skinny. He doesn't like the heat. He puked dog food up all over the yard yesterday. Nasty. Then today he didn't eat at all, so I gave him some cooked chicken. He gulped it down like he was starving! He didn't throw up so I guess he is OK. He has lost a lot of fur and looks even more "long funny." [Joshua's nickname for him. He says he is a long, funny dog.] *I will have to keep an eye on him to make sure he gets enough to eat. He just really doesn't like the heat. Me neither. It's been pretty cool this summer. At least in the mornings and evenings anyway. I have only had to turn on the air a few times. I open the house at night to cool it off and then close it up in the morning to keep the cool air in.*

*I took Chase to Grandma's house last week. He spent
the day being tormented by Louie. Louie would tease
Chase with the ball. If Chase tried to go for it, Louie
would nip him. It was a game for Louie, but not so
much for Chase.*

*Fino got the garden fence all the way done, I'll send
you a picture. Gotta go now - lots of housework to
do. I'll write again soon. Oh by the way, Fino said we
should get an internet house phone so you can call us.
I'll look into it. Take Care. Love, Mom*

I sent Joshua letter after letter, trying to fill his days. I didn't really
know what he needed most, so I tried to alternate between ordinary
and inspirational things. I wanted to be a light and a comfort to him.
I don't know, even now, whether or not I succeeded. I only know
that I tried, and that God took care of the rest.

Stained Glass Jesus

On August 22, 2011

Hi Mom,
*I got your letter about the garden. It didn't get here until
the 22nd. The mail room is kinda slow. Hey, by the way,
Happy 2nd Anniversary! You know that old saying, " If
you can make it two years, it might just work." LOL*

*Nothing's changed over here. I'm still stuck in Building
16. All Bad! I see people come in after me and leave
before me. I wouldn't really care, except I can't get
visits or canteen (the store). I can't cut my fingernails,
change my clothes or get a new razor. We have to share
shower shoes with the whole 200-man building. They
don't even give us cleaning supplies or full rolls of toilet*

paper. Oh, and no yard either (going outside). Even the hole (solitary confinement) has more action than 16. Not sure how much more I can stand. I think I'm gonna start pencil whipping the CDC (California Dept. of Corrections) with 602's (grievance forms). You know that old saying, "the pen is mightier than the sword." :) Anyways, that's life behind bars. :(

So Mom, I can't wait to hear the next chapter of your story. I have a story as well, but I'm waiting to write it and send it. It's what inspired the letter I wrote to Fino. Fino is a real great guy. He is always doing nice things for other people. I'm glad he helped out Teresa [another niece] *with her car. I would have been the one to help her probably, so I'm glad that Fino's around.*

Visits are on the weekend; I'm pretty sure but call and find out. Plus, make sure you ask what building I'm in cuz like I said, I can't get a visit in Building 16.

You finally paid the Jeep off, huh? I bet that was a relief.

Mom, I'm running out of things to read and do so can you send me a paperback puzzle book, or if you've got the money, go online and order me some paperbacks like Clive Cussler or Wilbur Smith. Anyways, love you lots. Write back. Love, Josh

P.S. The Catholic Chaplain stopped by and gave me this old book. The cover was a picture of Jesus done in stained glass, so I tore it off and put it in my window. When the sunshine comes through, I have a stained glass window. It looks pretty cool. :)

I was so touched by the stained glass Jesus that I got teary eyed. Only Jesus. Things that are grey and drab are illuminated and lit up by his presence. I don't know why Joshua was placed in the worst building in the entire prison, but I am suspecting it is so he will stop taking things for granted: freedom, family, even toilet paper. He has thrown away so many opportunities. Maybe God just wants to heal him of that and give him a heart that appreciates even the smallest things.

I think sometimes we forget how much we have and how much God can give us. I forget God's power. I weaken Him by my lack of faith. Then, He shows up in an unexpected way, like the stained glass Jesus and I am struck with the reality of His greatness and feel so sad that I doubted. A picture of Jesus in the window of a prison cell. It's like a doorway to heaven. Beautiful.

And then I wrote this.

If I could lift my eyes to see, enough to find your grace
Then in my window clear and bright would be my Savior's face
His glowing eyes look down with love, fulfilled by sunlit days
Forget me not oh, King of Kings, for I have gone astray

If I could lift my eyes to see before the path was lost
Perhaps my stained glass Jesus would not have paid the cost
For whom he came cannot be me, my value cannot hold
The beauty of his life cut short, death on the cross was told

If I could lift my eyes to see the hope that his face brings
Then glowing in my windowsill a place where hope now springs
Stained glass Jesus, Prince of Peace, a comfort in this place
Of nothingness and broken hearts that run a losing race

If I could lift my eyes to see, what joy my soul shall find
For Jesus Christ in faithfulness will ever now be mine
And so I kneel before my King, dirty floor beneath my knees
The beauty of my stained glass Jesus shining down on me

≈•≈

Out of Building 16

August 26, 2011

Hi Mom,
I have some good news for you. I finally got moved out
of Building 16. Normally, they send us to one of the
blocks that has cells. Instead, this time I got sent to the
gym. :) There's TV, yard, fans. We get to shower every
day. We even get to walk to chow. It's way better than
the cells. I'm doing much better now that I can move
around and breathe. I can also get visits now that I'm
in the gym. So, I'll be waiting to see you. Oh yea, just
a reminder, go ahead and call to see if you've been
approved and forget about the books. There's plenty to
read here. The puzzles would be nice. Grams sent me
some pictures of Grandpa. He sure was a handsome
guy, huh?

Tell Fino I like the resourcefulness of his pallet fence.
I thought that was a good idea. I'm glad to hear that
your garden is doing so well. If I were home I would eat
all the squash. I like that stuff. Well, I'm gonna go for
now. I hope to hear from you soon and see you as well.
Love, Josh

August 31, 2011

Dear Joshua,
I got your letter today saying that you are in the gym.
Great news! The day after I write "Stained Glass
Jesus," you get moved. Coincidence? I don't think so.
I sent you some 97 cent crossword puzzle books, word

*search, and soduko books. I sent a Readers Digest, too.
I already called to see if I am approved to visit. A lady
told me that I have to wait 6 weeks to get an approval
letter from the prison. I'll call again soon.*

*I wish you would have been here to eat the squash. I
had so much I was giving it away! It has slowed down
now. I guess that's why they call it Summer Squash. I
still have tomatoes, cantaloupe and pumpkins. They are
small, but tasty and help our food budget.*

*Fino has to work the Saturday of Labor Day Weekend,
so we'll go late to Aunt Trina's BBQ. (His schedule is
annoying sometimes.) The BBQ should be fun.*

*I have a picture of Grandpa that I am going to copy and
send to you. Except for the brown hair, it looks just like
you. Is that why you said in your letter that Grandpa
was a handsome guy?*

*It's been super hot here lately, over one hundred. Chase
has lost a lot of fur. I finally gave him a bath the other
day. He doesn't like baths and when he saw me turn on
the hose, he wouldn't come to me. He stood next to the
Pepper tree and just looked at me. Then, when his bath
was over, he rolled around in the grass. I guess he was
trying to rub the clean off. He's such a dork. Anyway, I
hope you like the poem I wrote. It was inspired by you.
Once again, I am glad you are in the gym and out of
Building 16. I will send another letter in a few days.
Take Care. Stay Strong. Love, Mom*

September 7, 2011

Dear Joshua,
We went to Aunt Trina's house for a Labor Day BBQ.
She had it with her new boyfriend, Clay. We swam
and ate chicken and stuff. Clay is pretty nice. He is
the brother of her best friend, Sue. I have known Sue
for years--as long as I've known Aunt Trina. I think
Aunt Trina felt guilty for dating Clay at first, but Uncle
Jimmy is not coming back and she is way too young to
spend the rest of her life alone.

I have had several housewares parties of my own. I'm
doing OK. I don't sell a lot of product, but enough, and
I get new bookings. I should make enough money to
help out. Also, Clay owns his own plumbing company
and has asked Fino to work for him on his days off. I
am not sure if it is good for Fino to always be working,
but just for a little while, he might have to. We need to
pay off some bills so we can get by a little easier. We
also want to eventually buy a house. Wouldn't that be
awesome! We should be ready just about the time you
get home. That way you can help us paint. I know how
much you love to paint!

Chase has a limp. Not sure what happened. It seems to
be worse in the morning when he first gets up, so it may
be arthritis. I feel bad for him and let him walk really
slowly on his way outside. Ryan was here the other
day. Chase was totally cool with him. No snapping or
anything. I guess he finally got used to him.

I'm working on a new play, a story loosely based on Uncle Harry and Aunt Margie. I called Uncle Harry and told him about it. He said he wants a copy of the script. Grandma said she wants to come see it. I wish you were here. You could help with the sets and stuff. You could sit with Grandma and watch it. It's pretty good. Pastor Teresa says I have a gift. Doesn't feel like a gift. It just feels the same as what I have always done, like eating breakfast or cleaning house or playing softball.

Anyway, I love you. Fino loves you too. He smiled when I read him the part in your letter where you said you liked his inventiveness in using the pallets to make a fence. He keeps saying he needs to write to you, but honestly, he hasn't even finished Danielle's birthday gift and her birthday was in June. He works late most nights and then works around the house the rest of the time. He barely gets a minute to breathe. He asks about you though. He misses you. He really misses his kids. I thought maybe we could go in November for his birthday. That would be cool. Well, I'm gonna close now. I will call today and see if Grandma and I can come visit you. I miss you. Fino probably can't come. He works on Saturdays. Love, Mom

This is How You "Pull a Joshua"

September 12, 2011

Dear Joshua,
I haven't heard from you in almost 2 weeks. I hope everything is OK. I hope you are just out of envelopes or stamps. This total lack of communication is kinda scary.

Not in a good Halloween kinda way, but in a real way. I called today to see if I was approved to visit. If so, I will be there as soon as I can manage it--finance wise and all. The gas to get down there is a bit of a hurdle. You know how it is from when you lived in Winchester and drove to San Diego for work. I thought maybe you had been moved, so I didn't write you any letters. I was waiting to get a letter from you saying that you had been sent somewhere else. I was told by prison staff that you are still there, so I decided to write again.

We are getting ready to go pick apples. It's that time of year again. Won't be the same without you. Aunt Trina might come and bring her new boyfriend. Fino and I have met him a couple of times.

Good News! They said I should have my approval to come visit by the end of next week. It's still a little ways off, but closer than I originally thought.

The latest on Nick: he got out of rehab and went to a sober living ranch--like the one you went to in Santee. The next day, I was baking a pie when I heard a knock on the front door. I opened it to find Nick standing there, carrying his bag of clothes and covered in sweat. I told him he pulled a "Joshua." He said, "What does that mean?" I told him the story of you making your way back to Grandma's house from that filthy place in Santee. Made us both laugh.

Please write back if you can. I am worried about you. I always think of you in the Fall, since it's the time of year for your birthday. Hey, maybe I can visit sometime around your birthday. That would be cool. I will send

*an envelope along in this letter like I did the last one.
I am short on money or I would put something on the
books for you. Maybe I can talk to Grandma and have
her put something on the books for you. I pray that you
are OK. We think and speak of you all the time. We love
you. Love, Mom*

This is how you pull a Joshua: We drove Joshua all the way from
North San Diego County out to a rehab facility in East San Diego
County. It was about an hour's drive. Joshua took a duffle bag full
of clothes and other personal items and got on a bus that would be
taking him the rest of the way to the facility. We waved to him until
the bus was out of sight. Keep in mind that this was a voluntary decision that Joshua made. After the bus drove away, we got into the car
and made our way back home. We stopped by my Mom's house to
let her know that Joshua had indeed gotten on the bus.

The next day, sometime in the early afternoon, my Mom heard a
knock on her door. When she opened it, there stood Joshua, sweat-
ing in the California heat, duffle bag in hand. He had burned a few
bridges, and being able to enter my mother's house again was one
of them. Seeing how hot and tired he was, she couldn't help herself,
and she let him inside. Joshua dropped his duffle bag on the floor
and followed her into the kitchen for a drink of water. He wanted
to know if he could use her phone to call me. She let him. When I
answered the phone, I was surprised to hear Joshua on the line. In
rehab, you are usually not allowed to make any phone calls until
several months have passed. When he told me that he was at his
Grandma's house, I said, "What happened?" Boy, did he ever have
a story to tell.

I guess the facility that he went to was basically a campsite. There
was no running water, just large buckets that they filled at a faucet
somewhere far from camp. They used it for EVERYTHING. Washing their hands, doing dishes. You name it. Most of the time, the
dishes didn't even get washed. They would just let the food dry on
them and re-use them. They were relieving themselves in the surrounding woods, and didn't have toilet paper. Most of the guys had

Hepatitis from IV drug use so the whole idea of not washing things was really getting to Joshua. They slept on cots with soiled mattresses, dirty pillows and sleeping bags. Joshua wouldn't take his clothes off to sleep. He even left his hooded sweatshirt on and pulled it up over his head so that none of his skin could make contact with the filthy bedding.

The next morning, he got up, packed his duffle bag and left. He walked to the main road and hitched a ride. He was picked up by an elderly Hispanic man in an old pick up. The man had a heavy accent and when he said Joshua's name it sounded like "Ya shu wa." Joshua said it sounded the way it would have been said in Bible times. The old man told Joshua that he wasn't supposed to be on that particular road; he was supposed to be at a prison in Mexico teaching Bible study. The prison had been locked down, so they had turned the man away. He said it was because God knew that Joshua would be there needing a ride.

As the two men rode along, Joshua shared his story about the dirty rehab facility and how he couldn't stay there, even though he really wanted to get clean and sober. The old man told him, "Ya shu wa, you could not stay in that dirty place because you are not a pig. Pigs are OK to stay in dirty places. That's what pigs do. But not sheep, Ya shu wa. Sheep do not like to be dirty. You are a sheep Ya shu wa. You are one of God's sheep." Joshua said he understood very well what the old man was telling him with this simple story.

When they reached a bus station, the old man handed Joshua some money and said, "This is all I have. Take it so you can go home." Joshua took the money, thanked the old man and walked towards the bus. He handed the bus driver the money and said that he needed to get as close to Escondido as he could. The bus driver counted the money. It was EXACTLY the right amount to take him all the way home. Joshua was stunned. To this day, he believes the old man who helped him was an angel. I believe it too. He got off the bus in Escondido, and on that hot summer day, walked the last 2 miles to his Grandma's house. After hearing this story from Joshua, I let him come back home. I believed that God was helping me to know when to be strong with Joshua and when to extend grace. This was a time to extend grace.

❧

And after a few more days with no letter, September 13, 2011, I wrote to Joshua again and said:

> *Dear Joshua,*
> *Grandma called me today and said she put $20.00 on your books. Don't spend it all in one place, OK? I still haven't received any word from you. I hope you are well. I called the prison to see if you were OK. They said you weren't on lock down and you weren't in Medical. I hope that means you are just out of stamps and envelopes. Remember, I will send you a stamp and envelope with each letter.*
>
> *Softball update: our team is in last place. We haven't won a single game. I finally started hitting again, after going through 4 games with only one base hit. Then last night, I just opened up and started hitting again. But, I also hurt my knee. Every time I stepped to throw the ball, my knee gave out on me. Not sure what that's all about. I did make a really good catch at first base! Everyone said I jumped up and snagged a line drive out of the air hit by a guy that was batting left-handed. Funny thing is that I have no memory of jumping. How does that happen? I kept asking Fino, "Are you sure I jumped?" It was weird. Oh well. At least I caught it, even if I was not aware of how I did it.*
>
> *We are working on a kids Christmas program at church. I have someone running it this year, so I don't have to do too much. That's really nice. Then after that, we start to work on Easter. We are doing another picture that comes to life. This time though, it is the famous painting of Jesus in the garden praying. It starts out looking like*

the picture then comes to life as he talks to his disciples.
Remember how they kept falling asleep? It's that story.
I just need someone who can act to play Jesus. We are
praying about that. Well, I have work to do. Take Care.
Write back soon. I miss you. Love, Mom

ॐ

At the Hotel California

Having not yet heard back from Joshua, on September
17, 2011, I wrote him another letter. It was a recap of the
letter I had previously written, catching him up on all the
activities around our house and asking him to write back.
And then, finally, the following day, I received this letter
from Joshua:

Dear Mom,
I'm sorry I haven't written to you in a while. I got trans-
ferred today to CRC in Norco, California. You know
the song by the Eagles "Hotel California." Well guess
what? That's where I'm at. Crazy, huh? I got some
good news and some bad news. The bad news is I'm
not at Jamestown and going to a Jamestown fire camp.
:(The good news is they have a camp here. That's why
I got sent here. I should be going there, but there's no
guarantee. Also, the camp's not like other camps. I will
still live in prison and get called to fire, instead of living
at camp. Oh well! However, I'm only about 1/2 hour up
the 15 freeway from you. :)

Mom, I'm also sending you my package list with this
first letter, so this one will be a little expensive, but
should be the only one for this much.

So Mom, I've been doing a lot of thinking and reading and I've got a lot of things to write to you about. I will begin as soon as I get a little more settled in. :) Hey, can you call Chris and let him know I've been moved? Also, I'm pretty sure that you should be approved to come visit here as well so I'll be waiting. Ha, ha, ha. Wait, I think that I'll send my package slip in the next letter. That way I can put more time and thought into it. Besides, I haven't even seen committee yet. OK, I'm back but the most important thing is that I want you to know I love you and miss you. Now you have my new #. Write back soon. Love, Josh

CA Rehabilitation Center, Norco – Hotel California

All the things we prayed about had come true. Joshua had been moved to Norco. It was a prison with a fire camp inside. He was only about a half hour drive from our house which meant I could go visit him regularly. He would also get to leave the prison periodically to go out and fight wild fires. This was the best of a bad situation.

His visitation days were every other weekend, first on Saturday and the next weekend, on Sunday. The visiting hours were from 7:30am to 2:30pm, though they made you leave around 2pm so they could process everyone out. There were vending machines and catered food from a fast food restaurant. The food was expensive, but well worth it when I saw how much Joshua enjoyed it. (I guess the food in the prison was really bad. This is how Josh described it, "You can squirt the mashed potatoes between your teeth, the vegetables are unrecognizable and the meat is runny. Mom, how do you make meat runny?" To which I replied, "I don't know Joshua, I don't know." We were only allowed to bring one dollar bills to spend on the food - I never really figured out why. We would either save them up (my Mom was really good at that) or go to the bank on Friday afternoon and get a stack of them.

Checking-in was the worst part of the visit. First of all, everything was outside, rain, wind, or shine. There was a long driveway that went past the prison on one side, and a sports park on the other. Weird. Why would you put a public sports park next door to a prison? Once you reached the end of the driveway, a guard would reach through the car window and hand you a form with a number on it for each person in the car. You would then park and take your form over to the sign in station. The higher your number, the longer you had to wait to get in.

You couldn't wear blue jeans or sleeveless shirts. Certain colors were off limits too. Any color that the guards (green and Khaki) or the inmates (blue and orange) wore were out. If you wore the wrong color or style, they would send you over to a visitor's assistance center where they would give you clothes to wear out of a grab bag. I tried to never make that mistake. Gross!

At the sign-in station you would complete your form with your name and the inmate's number and paperclip your driver's license to it. Then, you had to stand in line until it was your turn to be cleared by the guard at the desk. There were times when it took hours to get checked in. Once when my Mom was with me, I had to take her to the car and turn the heat on to keep her warm. We stood outside in the cold for so long, I was afraid it would affect her health. Another time, it was so foggy that they couldn't let the inmates out to walk to the visiting center. If they couldn't see them, there was a potential for trouble. Another time, there was a fight and the prison was locked down. One day, Joshua told me that a guy got stabbed and died. Horrible! Frightening! I still can't wrap my head around that. Your prison sentence becomes a death sentence? (It made me fearful for Joshua. I wanted my boy home.)

Once you made it past the first sign in station, you had to line up by a bench and take your shoes off for inspection. Then, on to another line to get scanned by a hand-held metal detector. After that, it was on to yet another line to wait to be let into the prison. The automatic gate opened and you walked into a fenced-in chamber. While the gate behind you slid shut, the gate in front of you would open. You would go through that gate and into a waiting room to be checked in *again,* then through another metal detector, out the back door, across a cement walkway, up the stairs and through the door to the visiting center.

But it wasn't over yet. There was a final check-in station where you handed over your driver's license and the completed form they had given you to keep until your visit was over. Staff called to the back to announce which inmate had a visitor. They assigned seats, and called the inmate while you waited for his arrival. The inmates all came in through a door at the far end of the visiting center.

This room, with the rows of seating areas and the door at the end of it, was the room I had seen in my vision. The one that I thought was an airport. Just like in my vision, Joshua would walk through the door looking strong and well, and smiling. I used to watch people's faces light up when they would see their inmate come through the door. Sweet, but sad. Children running to their Daddies, Mothers and Fathers hugging their sons, and wives embracing their husbands. There was an outside picnic area; we rarely went out there. In the fall when we first started visiting Joshua, it was too cold. Then later during the summer months, it was too hot. Many tables were not shaded by the patio cover. Joshua and I have very light skin and can sunburn in the space of about 10 minutes, so most visits were spent inside. It was noisy, with all the conversations that were going on around us, but it was so good to see Joshua and to talk to him in person, I hardly noticed. It was an old, run-down building and not very clean, but I was with my Joshua! That made it all OK.

One day when my Mom came with me, we played a board game—Yahtzee, I think--and for a little while, it seemed like old times, like we were at home, enjoying just being together. When I went there alone, Joshua and I would talk about private things, the kind of things he could only tell his Mother. I would listen and try to understand. Then, fire season started. Joshua had gone through training and his crew was being called out to fight fires, so I didn't get to see him for awhile. It was hard for me, but good for him. He would get to work hard during the day and sleep under the stars at night. He loved it. That's how the months at Norco went for Joshua and me.

The phone calls became infrequent. The letters did, too.

Sometime in September, in an undated letter, Joshua wrote to me. In a collect phone call just prior to his writing this letter, he had talked to me about placing an order for him through the prison store. He would send me a form with all the items he wished to purchase checked off. I could then go online and make those purchases for him and have the products shipped straight to him. It was the only way for him to have soap, socks, deodorant, or anything else for that matter. Before his arrest, Joshua had saved some money in a bank account. He asked me to get his debit card out of his belongings and use that money to purchase the items he needed. I used it to put money on the books for him in county jail. It wouldn't last much longer, but it had gotten him through up to this point.

> *Hi Mom,*
> *I changed my mind about sending the slip. I found out that the mail doesn't go out until Monday morning, so I had all weekend to think about it. The best way for you to order online is with a credit card. It will get to me faster that way. Hopefully before Oct 1st which is the next quarter. Can you go online and order this ASAP? That way I get it in September. The radio might have to wait, but the other stuff is essential. As I said, this one is the biggest order.*
>
> *When you go to the ATM, can you check how much money is left in my bank account? Thanks, Mom. Hey Lady, I'm sending you some more visiting forms. I'm not sure if you're cleared from the other prison, so call here and ask. If not, fill these out and send them back. Don't forget to fill one out for Grams.*
>
> *Radio - if you can figure out how to do the special purchase - Mom it sure would be nice to listen to music. :)*

I'm sure you understand. Love, Josh
P.S. Got to have music!!! Mom when you mail the visit
forms back send them to the P.O. Box.

Joshua's "Permanent" Prison Home

Society Deemed Me Unfit

*I received another letter from Joshua shortly thereafter,
on September 21, 2011:*

Hey Mom,

*It was great talking to you last night. :) It's been a while
since we've talked. I'm glad to hear that everything
hasn't stopped since I've been gone. For a moment
there, I thought the world would stop spinning. Hahaha-
ha!! I thought that was pretty funny when you told Nick
he pulled a Joshua. Mom, you should tell him that he
needs to take advantage of the time and opportunity he's
got right now. Otherwise, he could end up like me--stuck
in prison or worse... dead. Tell him I said that. What I
wouldn't give for that chance again. I blew my chance
over and over. Now I'm here squatting and coughing
until some cop says he's done staring at my butthole,
then raids the whole house. Fun, huh? That's what my
morning was like.*

*So Mom, let me get to the stuff I had mentioned during
our phone conversation. When I was stuck in the cell
in building 16, I was sitting there thinking I couldn't
believe the courts and society deemed me unfit to be free
to live amongst them, and I was feeling kind of bitter
about it saying to myself they were wrong and I can't
be that bad. Well, I learned in AA to stop being selfish*

and self-centered and look or reflect and see what my part in the whole situation was. At that point, I started reflecting on my whole life and all the times that I made a complete ass out of myself and the people I'm with. It was so bad in most cases that I had been asked to leave or been kicked out, etc. This would happen more often than not. I'm sure there are several instances that you can recall. That realization kinda shocked me. I thought, "Wow!" Maybe I'm not fit to live amongst society. Hmmm... "Well, of course I'm fit. I'm not that bad. I have a good heart, a bright smile, compassion and a helping hand." However, the recognition of a problem alone will not remedy it.

I need to figure out or find a way to combat or allevi-ate myself of the problem. That's one of the things I've come to realize. Funny how God works, huh? I have also come to understand that this time has been GIVEN to me not TAKEN from me. With that said, I now have a choice. What shall I do with this time? Kind of exciting. :) I wonder what sort of answers I can find. I'm thinking I'm gonna come out on top this time :) Anyway, that's where I'm at as of late. Thought I'd share that with you. Mom, thanks for everything. I hope to see you soon at a visit. Write back soon. Love, Josh

Starting All Over Again

On September 22, 2011 - after I had talked to Joshua via a collect phone call, I wrote this email to my Pastor:

Hi... Joshua is now in Norco (the place that the Eagles' song "Hotel California" is written about). You know...

"You can check out any time you like, but you can never leave." Of course that is where they would send him! It was a hotel once, back in the day. Now it's a prison. They are supposed to have a good drug rehab program. That could be a good thing. He has called me twice since arriving. He wants me to visit. I sent my visitation form in to Donovan when he was there. It takes 4 to 6 weeks to get approved. They moved him before that happened. Now, I have to start all over for the Norco facility. I am praying it goes through quickly. If not, it will be November before I can see him. He was super excited to tell me that we can hug and order food and have a meal together.

He had gotten ring worm from county jail. I asked him if he still had it. He said, "No." I said, "OK, then we can hug." (I was try-ing to make him laugh.) He seems to be in a really good mood, like the real Joshua. I used to ask him when he was in the middle of his abuse of drugs/alcohol, "Would the real Joshua please stand up?" Seems like he finally did. He really seems like himself, not some weird, demented version of who he thought he wanted to be. I'll keep you posted. Gayle

On September 22, 2011 I wrote to Joshua with the bad news of having to start the visitation approval process all over again:

Dear Joshua,
I called the prison and found out that I have to start over with the visitation approval process. UGH! I was excited about visiting, and was going to come this Sunday if money allowed. Now, I have to wait another 4 to 6 weeks. Well, I placed your order, radio and all. I sent in my visitation form. Hopefully, you will get them both quickly. I don't think Fino ever finished his visitation form. He was approved to visit Dawn [his ex-wife] when she was in jail. I didn't know the dates he was cleared for, so he was supposed to fill that

*part out. I don't think he did. Can you send me some
more forms just in case?*

*Keep me posted on whether or not you get actual calls
to fight fires. I'm not really sure I like the idea of you
being in the path of a wild fire, but I guess if it helps
the time pass for you, then it's OK. I will continue to
check on the status of my visitation approval. Grandma
wants to come too, but I think the first time, I would like
to come by myself. We can catch up and have a good
talk. It's harder to do that when there are more people.
I will bring Grandma next time. Also, can you send me
the stained glass Jesus? I want to have a friend paint
something from it. Call me again soon. Take Care.
Love, Mom*

❧

One day, I was driving down the 215 Freeway and I saw the sheep.
Do you remember reading Joshua's letter about the sheep? In Riverside County, they farm sheep. They move them from pasture to
pasture as they eat their way through the grass. Joshua felt a kinship
with the sheep as he seems to with all animals. He likened them to
the descriptions from the Bible of God's people. He felt like God
was trying to speak to him through seeing the sheep on seemingly
every road he was driving down. Well, this time, I was the one who
saw the sheep and I was reminded of Joshua's attachment to them.

The Sheep Are Back!

September 23, 2011

*Joshua,
It was so weird. I was at my friend's house around 5pm
on Thursday, telling her the story of the old Hispanic man
who gave you a ride on your way home from the rehab*

facility. Remember, that gross, dirty rehab facility? I was relaying the message he told you about being a sheep and not a pig, and about how pigs are OK living like pigs, but sheep are not. I explained how he gave you bus money for the trip home, and said your name the way it would be pronounced in Bible times, and how you thought he was an angel. My friend got chills. I said, "God speaks very clearly to Joshua."

Then later on, around 6pm, I was heading south on the 215 freeway and there they were! The sheep! Just like we used to see them in different areas, but we never saw them in transit. You said that you thought God was trying to tell you to come join His flock. The sheep were grazing in a field while the shepherd, with his sheep dogs nearby, was sitting in a chair watching over the flock. I couldn't believe it! I pulled over and got out of the car to take a picture. It didn't come out. The sheep blended in with the background and you couldn't tell they were there. Still, it was awesome! I wish you could have seen it.

Joshua (Ya shu wa), never take for granted how God works so hard to communicate with you. Most people never see or hear what you see and hear. He pulls back the curtain that separates us from the Holy of Holies to show you He is real and to show you His promises. He speaks clearly and powerfully to you. He adores you. You are part of His flock even though you stray.

Remember the story about the shepherd breaking the leg of the lamb that kept wandering off? Remember that you broke your foot? Remember the vision of the angels and demons fighting in the sky in Grandma's backyard while the light of the cross was shining?

*For all of us, for you, and for me, now is the time for us
to choose whom we will serve. As for me and my house,
we will serve the Lord.*

I love you Joshua.

૭૦૦૬

It's Officially Fall Now

September 25, 2011

*Dear Joshua,
You are right. You have a good heart, a bright smile,
compassion and a helping hand. That's a pretty good
skill set. You write well and have a really good sense of
humor. You are loyal and devoted. I know how hard it is
to objectively look at your own shortcomings. Believe
me; I have had to do it many times myself. It really is
the only way to improve. But just think of it this way:
all you have to do is modify your behavior. You don't
have to learn compassion, or grow a tender heart, you
already have those. You just need to lead with them.
Always put your good heart and your bright smile out
there first, and keep them there. I told Nick what you
said about him taking advantage of the opportunity he
has been given. He smiled and said, "OK."*

*I could never work at a prison. What if I were assigned
the duty of being "butthole checker???" I would barf.
I would rather flip burgers for the rest of my life than
check buttholes even once. Who cares about retirement,
insurance or salary. Some things just aren't worth it!
Period! I hope life settles in for you. I hope I get to*

come visit soon. Maybe by some miracle, the 4 to 6 weeks it takes to get approved will be shortened. That would be cool.

It is officially Fall as of September 21st. The weather has cooled down a lot. It's overcast in the morning and the highest temperature is in the 80's. I'm loving it. Chase is too. He doesn't like the heat.

Did I tell you about my knee? We were playing a softball game. Our first baseman was hurt, so I had to play first. I caught a ball thrown to me. The runner was out. The runner who had been on second tried to run to third. He took two steps off of the base, and I threw the ball to second to stop him. As I did, I pushed off with my right leg and stepped forward on my left. I felt a terrible pain in my right knee. I grabbed it and limped around a little, but the game must go on, so I got ready for the next batter. Once again, the shortstop threw the ball to me at first and we got the runner out. On the hit, the runner who had been on second ran to third. As I caught the throw from shortstop, I saw him round third and head for home. He, again, only took a few short steps. I threw the ball to third to try to get him out. There was the stabbing pain in my knee again. At home, after the game, I noticed some swelling in my knee. I got some ice, placed it on my knee and wrapped it. I kept it there all night. It didn't work; it was still swollen the next day. It's been two weeks and my knee is still pretty sore. I played a game last week with a knee brace. All I could do was stand at home plate and catch. It will probably be the same this week. Fino said he thinks I need to warm up more before each game. I told him I think I just need to be younger.

*Today is Monday. I am going over to my friend's house
to help her sew. She has a bunch of clothes she is making and is close to her completion deadline. She is a
little behind and asked me to help. She said she will pay
me. I don't really like to sew, but she is my friend and
we could use the extra money. I will close for now. Take
Care. Keep Smiling. Love, Mom*

Every Fall for more than 20 years, my kids and I have gone apple
picking. Over the years, different family members would join us.
Usually, it was my Mom, my Daughter, Joshua, and me. One year,
Joshua thought my Mom threw an apple at him. He was young, in
elementary school. I had him on my shoulders and he was reaching
up to grab an apple from one of the top branches. As he pulled the
apple off, the branch snapped back up, causing several other apples
to fall off. One of them hit him in the head. His story was, "I saw
Grandma's hand go up and right after that an apple hit me in the
head." He teasingly torments my Mom with that story even now.
I always laugh and say, "Right, Josh, because Grandma is so mean
that she throws apples at her grandkids." Even after my kids were
grown, we picked apples together in the Fall. As the years passed,
we took my grandkids too. The only year we didn't go was the year
my Father died. His birthday was in September. None of us had the
heart to make the trip that year.

Happy Birthday, Joshua!

September 30, 2011 - Joshua's birthday is October 7th. As a gift, I
wrote him a letter detailing some of the events of his first year of
life. At 2 weeks old, he had surgery on his stomach. Pylorex Steno-
sis was the medical diagnosis. It's a valve at the bottom of your
stomach that allows food to pass to your intestines. Joshua's was
elongated and would not open. It caused projectile vomiting. He
threw up the first time on a Wednesday evening, the day he turned
2 weeks old. I called the doctor that next morning, Thursday. They
said that babies sometimes throw up, but that if it happened again,

I should bring him in right away. I knew that something was really wrong, but did as instructed. I fed him water, as it seemed to be the only thing he could keep down. When he threw up the next morning, I loaded him into the car and took him to the Doctor. I didn't even bother to call first. When I got there, the Doctor asked me to feed him and then watched Joshua vomit. It was awful. By Friday night, Joshua was at the hospital being prepped for surgery. It was a very scary time for me, but also served to bond me to Joshua in a very special way.

Dear Joshua,

I was cooking roast beef and carrots today. I found a carrot that still had some green on top. In your honor, I decided to put it in some water and see if it would grow. I'll keep you posted. It's almost your birthday. It doesn't seem like it was 30 years ago that you were born. Seems like it was just yesterday. I can remember it like it was yesterday. The first time I held you I said, "Hello little Buddy." I guess it (our friendship) started right then. It was a great day. You were born in the morning, on your due date. That hardly ever happens. Most of the time the doctor will give a date and the birth will happen somewhere near that time. Not you. You never do anything like anyone else, even being born.

From the very first moments of your life, you were fascinating! Your hair, your skin, your personality, everything was unique. You didn't look like your sister, or me, or Dale [his Father]. *You looked like you, and you were so peaceful. You never cried. I used to have to make sure you ate every 4 hours just to be safe, because you didn't even cry when you were hungry. You just kind of made soft noises. If I weren't listening closely, I would miss it.*

*When you were 2 weeks old and went to the hospital
for surgery, they had to pump your stomach. You were
hungry, but I couldn't feed you. You had to have an
empty stomach for the surgery. You were supposed to
go to surgery at 6pm, but there was a car accident and
they had to use the operating room for a young girl with
a ruptured spleen. You had to wait until 8pm, hungry
all the while. You cried and cried. It was so unlike you.
It was killing me. The only time you would stop crying
is when I held you and talked to you. As long as I was
talking, you would stay calm. If I stopped, you would
start to cry again. I held you and talked for 2 and 1/2
hours.*

*You were so small. It was so scary. I was worried about
the anesthesia. I couldn't imagine how they could put
a tiny baby under anesthesia and be sure they could
wake him. I asked the doctor about it. He tried to make
me feel better, but it didn't work. I remember my friend
Linda came up to the hospital. She was worried about
you and me. I was crying and really tired when she got
there. At one point, she had to help me stand up. My
knees just buckled beneath me. I think it was when they
were putting in your I.V., you were crying because it
hurt and the thought of it made me feel weak, like I was
going to faint.*

*Funny thing was, after the surgery, you looked perfectly
well. Your recovery was so fast! You had stitches in your
stomach and an I.V. in the large vein in your head. It
was the only place they could find a vein big enough. I
had to be really careful when I held you so that I didn't
hurt you. I could only feed you 2 ounces at a time. You
didn't cry very much. You would kinda make your same*

*soft noises. I had to make sure you burped really well,
too. The nurses said a gas bubble would be very painful
for you, so I would feed you and then carefully burp
you. I couldn't touch your stomach. Then, I had to wait
about a half an hour and feed you again. This was all
while you were in the hospital. I remember too, that
since I didn't have a car, I had to walk to the hospital to
see you, then walk back home afterwards. You lost some
weight because of the surgery, so you looked a little
skinny for awhile, especially when you came home and
I saw you next to your sister. She was always a chunky
little thing. You gained weight slowly. You didn't really
catch back up until you were a toddler. You walked
early so I guess you were just under a year old, before
you finally filled out completely.*

*It was a great first year, minus the surgery part. You
were fun and sweet and so cute. I carried you everywhere. You would hold on tight and I would vacuum,
do laundry-- everything except cook dinner--with you
on my hip. You were perfectly happy that way! You only
really liked Grandma, your sister, and me. You weren't
interested in anyone else. When you were a little older,
you didn't want to learn to talk, partly because your sister always talked for you and waited on you hand and
foot, but also because it's just part of your personality
to observe the world more than to comment on it. You
were just taking it all in.*

*I just wanted to share with you some of the memories
I have from 30 years ago when you were born. Truly,
there are 3 days that stand out in my mind so clearly
that time does not diminish them. They are, not in any
particular order, the day your sister was born, the day*

you were born, and the day I married Fino. Those days are beyond a doubt, the 3 best days of my life. I'm smiling now just thinking about them.

Happy Birthday, Joshua. Love, Mom

Jail House Thievery

October 6, 2011

Hi Mom,
Last night, I got the letter about when I was a newborn. I thought it was great! :) Better than some generic card. You certainly have a flair for writing. I said in a letter to Fino I would explain what brought those words out. (Not sure if you've read it or not.)

So here's the deal: when I was in Building 16, my cellie didn't receive a razor in his fish roll, but I did. Well, he started growing a beard. I was shaving. He'd never grown a beard before. It started to drive him crazy, the itching and all. One night, I go to sleep and I keep hearing this water hitting the basin of a stainless steel sink. Not quite loud enough to wake me up, but just annoying enough to rouse me from my slumber. When I woke, I didn't jump up or move right way. I stayed still and tried to recognize what on earth that sound could be. A few days prior to this when I was shaving with the dull razor, he said to me that it would help if I soaked my face first with a hot towel. Then it dawned on me, that's what he was doing. I couldn't believe it! When I rolled over to see if my razor was sitting on the shelf where I left it, of course it wasn't there (oh my gosh)! He did some shuffling around and acted like he was washing his arm pits—"the onions." LOL.

I'm not sure if you're aware of this fact or not, but jail house thievery is absolutely unacceptable. The consequences can be life threatening. My first reaction is disbelief, like "Oh my gosh... No way!" But, it's right there in front of my face. I start to brew and get angry. As I'm hopping down off of my rack, I say to him, "Did you do what I think you did?" He says something along the lines of, "Huh?" By now I'm almost steaming with anger. My mind's going a hundred miles an hour with thoughts. Is this guy really that bold? I'm gonna have to pound this guys face in, I'm gonna go to the hole, get more time, get new charges, fire camp's out of the question if I hit him. It's all bad. These are a few of the thoughts--all negative.

By now I'm standing on the stool at the table, and he is moving about kinda funny, a little shifty, like when a little kid gets caught doing something wrong. He hurries and sits down on his rack. I say to him, "What about your career?" More like I'm saying it aloud to myself cuz I'm still kind of shocked but at the same time saying it to him. When I say, "career," I mean prison career. That's what convicts call it. It basically means you're solid and not a rat, snitch, child molester, etc. I'm pacing the floor and he is sitting on his rack kinda in the corner with his back to the wall (a way he never sits). I'm standing at the opposite end of the cell by the door. I mutter things like, "Wow! I can't believe this, and "that's your career." I'm still reeling from the whole situation. I pace a few more times. I can see he's getting quite nervous. I'm not a mean person by nature. You know, I don't want to ruin this kid's career and rearrange his face, but the rules in prison say otherwise. I'm not sure what to do here. I'm at a loss for an

*answer... hmmmmm... I grab my Bible. The little pocket
one. New Testament, Psalms, Proverbs. I walk back
to my corner of the ring, but now I'm armed with the
Word. I begin flipping pages looking for the answer. The
tension is still so thick you could cut it with a knife.
As I'm searching, I'm saying, "That's your career."
Pause for a moment then say, "Did you take me for a
fool or think I'm weak?" He's saying, "What's wrong
Josh? You're acting funny" and "Come on, can we talk
about this?" Still searching out the answer, reading different passages here and there. "Come on Josh, what's
up, man?" he says. I'm still searching. I'm expecting
the answer to jump out and find me. It doesn't. However,
I begin to speak. Not sure of what I'm saying, or where
I'm going with it, but listening intently as the words
flow from my mouth. It was the voice of reason and
authority. I was thinking, "This is strange." I felt as if I
rose in stature and my voice became deeper, almost as if
the bass from it went through to the bone.*

*My cellie was sitting now, with the look of a child,
eager to learn. He then pops up, grabs the razor that
he threw under the bed, turns to me with it in his hand,
and apologizes. We stood face-to-face for a moment,
not saying a word. You could hear a pin drop. I broke
the silence and said, "Why don't you have a seat." He
sits down with his head hung low. I say, "I'm glad you
chose to come clean." I begin to speak again with the
voice of authority. All the while, I have the book open
and continually glance at it as I flip through the pages.
As I'm speaking, he begins to cry. I say to him, "It will
all be OK." Then as I hold the book up and shake it
in my hand, I say, "This will someday save your life."
I said, "I'm not the weak, I'm the strong. Trust in the*

Lord." He lifted his head. I said, "I forgive you. Let's not speak of this again." He agreed.

We shook hands and spoke as friends the rest of the night. I told him he still needs to be punished. I said his punishment will be that he has to grow a beard! We both thought that was very fitting and had a laugh. It's amazing how God works. He's got a certain unpredictable randomness in getting the point across. So there. That's my story Mom. I've got a few more that I will send soon. Mom, I'm sending a package form with this letter. I know it's kinda expensive, but you only have to get it once. Love, Josh

After I read this letter, all I could think was, "Wow!" God was really speaking to Joshua (and through Joshua), and changing him. I hoped and prayed that after so many times in and out of trouble, this would be his last. It sure seemed that way.

October 13 and 14, 2011 - I wrote two short letters to Joshua back to back. Here are the condensed versions:

Dear Joshua,
I got your letter, the order form, and the photo. Thank you! I really like the story you sent. It had so many things in it that popped off the page. I like the way you write because it's very real, very honest. It paints a clear picture of what you are feeling and what life is like being locked up. It is sometimes difficult for me to read. I don't ever want you to be in ugly, unpleasant situations. I guess parents (Moms) want their kids to have the best of everything. I am happy that you share your experiences with me. It helps me to know you better and to stay close to you.

I sure miss you Joshua. I miss arguing with you and watching you play with the dogs: all the good stuff! Love, Mom

Dear Joshua,
My bird of paradise died. I'm so bummed. It's the one you got me for Mother's Day (right before your arrest). I kept trying things to get it to live, but it looked like it had a mold or something. There was weird black stuff on it. I'm going to buy a new one to replace it and pretend it never died.

I looked up the prison where you are being held. The computer has a picture of it from a satellite or something. I can see the sports park next to it. (In a phone call, he told me he could hear the crowds and smell the nachos at the softball/baseball fields next door.) No wonder you can hear the sound of the games. I'm glad you get to hear normal things now and then. At least you're not totally cut off from the rest of us. I tried to call today to see if I am approved to visit; the phone just rang and rang. I will keep trying. I'll get there eventually, whether you like it or not! Haha! Love, Mom

I Cradle You

October 15, 2011 - I wrote a poem for Joshua and sent it to him with this letter:

Dear Joshua,
I wrote you a poem today. I got to thinking how, for the child, life changes. They grow, become an adult. For the mother, too, the child changes... they grow up,

but the feeling of wanting to comfort and cradle them never changes. We just have to hold it inside. The infant is kissed and rocked. The adult is held in treasured memories.

I hope you are well. Remember that Joseph was in jail for 12 years. He survived. He did not become a criminal. He remained faithful to God, and for his faithfulness, God kept him safe and rewarded him.

Stay in the Word. Keep your mind on what is good and what is pure. God didn't give you a spirit of fear, but of strength and love and a sound mind. Your hope for a new beginning, a new day, is Christ. He WILL deliver you from despair, pain, fear and heartbreak, from every dark thing that haunts your thoughts. He can and WILL restore you. Let him. Trust him. When you don't know what to do, He does. When you don't know what the future holds, He does. When you don't know what the answer is, He does. He is the I AM. He is all you need. He is clarity. He is sanity. He is your defense and your provider. His love never fails. He remains faithful always. He will never leave you. He will uphold you. He keeps His promises. You are one of them. Your life is full of promise. The future is a clean slate. Let the creator of the universe, the one who has placed the stars and made the whole world, take you where He wants you to go. You will find that it is where you had always hoped to be anyway. A dream come true.

As you seek out the Lord, you are in my heart, in my mind and in my prayers. I love you. I cradle you. With Love, Mom

I cradle you
In darkest night, by light of day
Your tiny hands, your gentle cry
With all my heart
I cradle you

I cradle you
In thoughts that last throughout the day
While I work, while you play
With all my mind
I cradle you

I cradle you
I sit and wait through sleepless nights until the break of day
Hoping for your safe return
With all my love
I cradle you

I cradle you
From distances that span between, of missing you each day
I send my prayers to keep you safe
With all my soul
I cradle you

Stressed Out Again!

October 24, 2011 - After not receiving any letters from
Joshua for a while, I finally received this one:

Hi Mom,
I'm writing because I'm stressed out again. Sometimes,
just writing makes me feel better. I'm not really sure where

I'm gonna go with this, but it beats sitting here being frustrated about things that I have no control over, right? I get sick of having to deal with a bunch of idiots. I'm not sure you could ever know this pain of mine, one you think I'd be well equipped to overcome, being that I keep ending up in this situation. It's very hard to be positive in such a negative environment. This place is supposed to be about respect; however, it's not. I think it's cause everyone is so self centered, not just in here, but all over the world. Mom, I must admit you've done a fine job bringing me up. Even with all my faults and shortcomings, I'm a kindhearted, respectful, caring person. Thanks, Lady. :) I can only hope that I can hold up, almost like a front, you know, a tough guy image, long enough to make it through this time. I find the tough guy image is not me, and I don't feel comfortable acting like someone I'm not. Well Mom, the show must go on. I will talk to you later. Love you lots, Josh

P.S. Wish me luck, or tell me to break a leg or whatever it is you actors say.

(I used to run the Drama Department at our church and have performed in a few plays myself, so his "break a leg" comment was a cute reference to that. Plus my kids always call me a Drama Queen!)

October 29, 2011

Dear Joshua,
I love your letters! They always have something in them that makes me smile. By the way, "Break a leg!" Sorry you're in such a rotten place. Wish you weren't, that's for sure. Can't wait until I can visit.

My new kitten is here. His name is Squishee. I was told that he is 5 weeks old, but I don't think that is correct. He can't eat solid food or find the litter box on his own. He seems more like 4 weeks. I had to buy formula for him. It is called Step 2 because it is supposed to help kittens go from nursing to solid food. I mix it up, so it is very thick, and then coat his hard food with it until it softens. I have to feed it to him piece by piece. If I don't, he just licks everything. He has a daily routine. He wakes up, goes to the bathroom, plays for a little while, eats and goes back to sleep. He does it every 4 hours. Just like a human baby! I get up and feed him and clean him up every 4 hours. He tries to clean himself, but he isn't very good at it; he loses his balance and falls over.

Chase doesn't know what to think of him. He freaks out when he meows. He gets fixated on the kitten and I'm afraid he is going to eat him. I give them short amounts of time together every day to familiarize them with one another. This is all a really big hassle, but Squishee is very soft and squishy, so it's OK. He likes to sleep on our shoulder or chest. Fino plays with him too, even though he said, "He's gonna be squishee all right." He's just teasing, but I told him he better not hurt my kitty! I sent some pictures of him. He is an orange tabby, not like Feats [our other cat], with some white, but all orange stripes. He is super cute. I have to take him to the Vet and get him his shots and also snipped.

I might have to have surgery on my knee. It's still not better. I can stand on it, but I can't bend it. I am going to the doctor on Wednesday. So, I am done with softball for good. I can't afford to be injured. I guess it was a good run. I started when I was 9 and played until I was 51.

Keep those letters coming. They cheer me up. When I
don't hear from you for awhile, I really start missing you.
I miss you anyway, but when you don't write, it's worse.
Stay strong. Keep up the acting! (At least until you come
home, then you can just be yourself.) We like you when
you're being you--caring and funny! Love, Mom

It was strange and interesting that during the time referenced in the letters above, God had given me a vision of Joshua trapped inside a plaster coating. He was posed and unable to move. Slowly, small cracks began to show in the plaster. Small pieces began to chip off and fall to the ground. It was similar to a baby bird breaking out of an egg. Then with one final burst, Joshua broke completely out of the cast and was free. As he wrote, I began to see that reality take shape.

October 31, 2011

Dear Joshua,
God will make a way for you to endure. I know he will.
You're right; I don't know how awful it is for you. I know
that I don't want you to be where you are. I know that you
should be in a better place, a better life. I know that you
will be someday. The time you spent (in prison) will be
nothing more than a story to tell. It will no longer be your
reality. Until then, God will make a way. When we are
weak, He is strong. When we reach the end of the rope,
He throws us a lifeline. Like Daniel in the Lion's den, God
will make a way. Look for it. Remember, nothing happens
to you as a Christian by chance. It's all prearranged by
God. Look for His plan. The Bible says, "Ask and you
shall be given, seek and you shall find, knock and the door
shall be opened for you."

God will make a way. :) Love, Mom

And then, all of a sudden, I was approved to visit. I could hardly wait to go see Joshua. I think I missed him more than a parent would normally miss one of their children in their thirties. My guess is I had not completely recovered from my fear of losing him. Because of his high risk behavior, I was still dealing with a heightened sense of anxiety and fear over his well-being. I talked to Joshua on the phone a few times. He tried to give me the inside scoop for visiting. His information helped a lot. As time passed, and visiting Joshua became routine, I learned the ins-and-outs of what to do, but for that first visit, I was pretty nervous.

November 13, 2011 - After our visit, Joshua spent a lot of time in training, getting ready for the upcoming fire season. I didn't get many letters from him. He couldn't call our cell phones collect, so if he needed to communicate anything to me, he would call my Mom's house and ask her to relay information to me. I still wrote to Joshua though. He was always in my thoughts and prayers. Letters were simply an extension of that.

> *Dear Joshua,*
> *I just got home from my visit with you. It was so good*
> *to see you. You looked healthy, strong and clear eyed.*
> *I wish we could have had more time, but that is OK.*
> *Everything happens for a reason and in the proper time.*
> *No coincidences. I did notice a bit of darkness creeping*
> *in. Your walk with the Lord seems to have stalled out.*
> *Don't let that happen. Don't let go. As I was driving*
> *home, I began to pray for you. It came out like this:*

> **Prayer for Joshua**
> *Dear Lord,*
> *Close his eyes to the injustice around him and instead,*
> *teach him to pray for justice to reign. Close his eyes to*
> *the deceitful, treacherous way of men and instead, show*
> *him honesty and integrity in unexpected places. Close*
> *his eyes to arrogance and anger and instead help him*

to speak your words of healing into the place of insecurity and hurt from where the arrogance and anger spout. Close his eyes to the cruelty of men and instead, give him a heart of compassion. Close his eyes to the ugliness he has seen and instead show him beauty. Close his eyes to any trick or plot the enemy might use to destroy him. Let tricks or enemies have no impact and leave no scar. Give him a renewed mind and a fresh outlook. Restore him to the innocence of his youth and open his eyes to the knowledge that your love, sacrifice, mercy, and grace are overwhelmingly more than he needs to get through every minute, of every hour, of every day, for the rest of his life.

In Jesus' Name, Amen.

You are deeply loved, constantly prayed for, often thought of, and worthy of grace. Love, Mom

૭∽૭

Tough Turkey Day

On November 27, 2011 - Joshua finally had a moment of down time and wrote:

Hi Mom,
It was so great to see you the other day. :) Sorry I haven't written sooner. They keep us pretty busy around here. I hope you can make it back soon for another visit. My visiting days for December are Sunday the 11th and Saturday the 24th. However, I'm not sure you will want to waste your Christmas Eve coming to see me in prison. Mom, what I was really thinking is that you should just wait until next month and save your money.

*That way you can buy more Christmas gifts for every-
one. It's not like I'm going anywhere. So Lady, I must
admit, I think this Turkey Day was the worst I've ever
spent in prison. It's never hit me like this. I woke up like
normal as if I were home. I hung around the "house"
for a bit. I could almost hear you nagging at me saying,
"You better get ready or we're leaving without you."
So, I went and took a shower and shaved. I got dressed
up in my Sunday best. Then I realized, I had nowhere to
go or anyone to spend Thanksgiving with. I never felt so
far from home. I really do enjoy spending the holidays
with my family. I've been doing it my whole life.*

*This one's hitting hard Mom. There's still good in it
though. I'm finding out what kind of things really matter
to me. Mom, I don't want you to think I'm falling away,
again. My time is more occupied is all, and besides, I
spend my time with God in my own special way. After
all, I am quite unique. :) Love, Josh*

After reading this letter, my heart broke a little bit. It's pretty tough
to know your child is hurting and not be able to do anything about
it; but with God, there are no wasted moments. It all works for the
good. Knowing that kept me going. There were things Joshua needed
to learn and God is an excellent teacher. I had to trust that he would
take Josh to the place where he needed to be without irretrievably
breaking his heart. Even if it felt like it was breaking mine.

Fung Shway?

November 29, 2011

*Dear Joshua,
I enjoyed your last letter, except the part about me nagging you! And you are definitely unique... I will give you*

that! I will come visit you on December 24th. My knee should be pretty well healed by then. I have to sing for the Christmas Eve Service, but if I organize my clothes and meals the day before, I should be able to get where I need to be, so I can see you and make my mic check. Aunt Trina and her boyfriend Clay are coming to hear me sing. Oh... by the way, I finally got Fino to complete a visitation form, so maybe he can come with me to see you in January.

You know, he is so funny. I never know what I am going to find when I come home. For example, he went to the doctor and had him run labs on his blood sugar, cholesterol... you know, a full work up. His sugar was a little high as was his cholesterol. It can all be controlled by diet so I changed a few things on my shopping list to accommodate that. I bought him some reduced-sugar candy bars, that way he can still have treats. I came home from the store one day and found him sitting on the couch dipping the reduced sugar candy bars in the whipped cream topping that was left over from Thanksgiving! He said the candy bars didn't taste very good so he dipped them in the whipped topping. I guess he doesn't fully understand the concept of controlling his diet!

When you were a kid, I made you spend the holidays with family for a reason. There was a plan. I was trying to teach you the value of being invested in and committed to people, family. Relationships are what give life meaning. It's why we are here. I wanted you to have roots, to know where you came from, so you could figure out where you wanted to go. The Bible says that as we mature, we return to the things we were raised

*with. And besides, your family loves you. I wanted you
to have that to take with you no matter where you went.
I am a little bit nervous about this surgery I am having on my knee. I am never comfortable with being
knocked out and being cut into. Things are usually OK,
but there's always a slim chance something could go
wrong. I don't have much choice. You saw how I was
limping. Here's the weird part: it's my right knee, and
I'm right-legged. It sounds strange, but every time I
try to step up on a stair or something similar, I initially
start with my right leg, and then realize it hurts. I have
to stop and think how to do the same movement leading
with my left leg. It's like being right-handed and trying
to write with your left hand. It throws off my fung shway
(not sure how to spell that, but you know what I mean).
I am scared I am going to trip over something too. I am
so unsteady now; if a little kid bumps into me or a dog
makes an abrupt stop in front of me, I topple over. It's
horrible.*

*That's my update for now. I am really sorry that you
missed us on Thanksgiving. It's hard for me to know
that you are hurting and I can't do anything about it,
but we'll get through it. I will visit as much as I can
and then you will be home one day. I hope you have a
wonderful day today and know that I love you and that
God loves you. Take Care. Love, Mom*

Every other weekend I would visit Joshua. It was nice to enjoy time
with him - just me and my Buddy. Christmas came and went. I did
go see him on Christmas Eve. I took my Mom with me too. Joshua
really loves her! It wasn't the same as having him with us on Christmas day, but I knew this was not a permanent situation. He would
be home one day and we would spend as much time together as we

wanted. Once the holidays were over and our lives slowed down, I got back to my regular routine of writing to Joshua. The new year was upon us which meant that Joshua was that much closer to coming home.

January 4, 2012

Dear Joshua,

I know it's been a long time since I have written. The holidays were crazy busy. Plus, I got to see you, so I felt I didn't have as much to write to you about. Didn't we have fun on Christmas Eve? There were moments when I forgot where we were. Seemed we were simply hanging out playing board games. I had a great time and really enjoyed myself. Grandma did too! I will bring her again sometime. I don't want you to get lonely!

So, now Fino is not working. He is on unemployment. He looks for work and volunteers at the church. We have more buildings now so Raul can't get to all the work. It keeps him busy. It's better than sitting around the house bored. How are you? I know you said you are much busier than before. That's a good thing. Have you started your fire fighting classes yet? You will do well, I know. How long do the classes last? You can't go out to fires until you pass the class, right? I am not sure I like you out on fires. It scares me. Fire scares me! But I know that you aren't afraid, so I guess I just need to deal with it. :) You should become a fire fighter when you get out. That would be a good career for you. It seems like you'd like it too. Kinda exciting. Anyway, I'm gonna take Fino his lunch now. I hope you are doing well. I think of you and pray for you every day. You are never forgotten. Love, Mom

The letters from me to Joshua continued to flow. The letters from Joshua stopped. He was busy fighting fires and working around camp. In the outside world, Joshua is an electrician. He is very skilled in many other areas and very mechanically inclined. What he doesn't know how to do, he can figure out. Once the guards found out that he could do so many different things, they had him working all over the prison. He built a retaining wall, fixed the electrical... the list goes on and on.

I continued to write. He continued to not write. That was OK.

Hope For The Future

January 11, 2012

Dear Joshua,
It was fun visiting with you on Sunday. Like I said about Christmas, some of the time, it didn't feel like we were in a prison. Just seemed like we were hanging out some-where talking.

You look really good. I like it when your eyes are clear and you have some meat on your bones. You have pretty eyes. They are a nice shade of green. When they are clear they have a lot of laughter and joy in them.

The verse we talked about at our visit, "I know the plans I have for you, declares the Lord. Plans to pros-per you and not harm you. Plans to give you hope and a future." (Jeremiah 29:11) God doesn't declare things for no reason, He declares them with purpose when He wants to make a point. It is a statement of fact, like when the kings in Old England sent out a declaration. It was a done deal. It was law, it would happen.

Sometimes, it is hard to see that God's plans are for good. Think about it... Fino and I both out of work. We were so stressed trying to figure out why and what to do. While I was praying, I heard what seemed like an audible voice say, "I cannot build on a weak foundation. I have to tear down the old in order to build the new." Fino wants to be a pastor. He would never have quit his job on his own, but since they laid him off, he has a chance to volunteer at the church. The only people who ever get hired on staff are those who volunteer first. Additionally, he has been taking online classes to get a Theology degree.

I know when you look at your future, you see all the roadblocks to overcome; but if you hadn't been detoured from the road you were on, you may not have survived. God spared your life. I know the jail time you've been given seems long and impossible to endure, but you need time to make a complete, once and for all, life-altering change. God gave you time. I am not saying I like you being in jail. I'm not happy about it at all. I have a hope that God has plans for your future.

Do this for me just cuz I'm asking you to: look at your life as if you have a brand new beginning, a clean slate. You have been completely pardoned of your wrongdoings. Nothing is being held against you. You can do anything you want. Your dreams from childhood can be realized. The world is your oyster. You have unlimited access to finances, education, relationships... everything. What would you do?

Everyday from this point on, do one thing that will get you closer to your goals. And Pray. Ask God to bless you. It works. I have firsthand knowledge that it works. One day while Fino was praying, he felt like God spoke to him and said, "Write your dreams down, so I can bless them." He did, not knowing what would come of it, or why it was important to write them down. With the way things have turned out, it makes pretty good sense. He wrote down that he wanted to be involved in the men's ministry and to go to school. All that has happened. And me, I get to run a performing arts school. I love it.

I don't know what your level of faith is at this point, but just trust God, like when you went bungee jumping at the fair. Let go and trust that the cord will hold you-- that God will hold you. I know you feel like you have nothing to back your faith up, but you do. Remember all the times that God sent you help when you needed it the most? Remember back on all the times He saved your life? You have asked Christ into your heart. He said that if we do that, He will never leave us. He kept His word, Joshua. He has never left you. Find your place and let God take you there. Love, Mom

Grandpa

January 19, 2012

Dear Joshua,
I found this picture of Grandpa back when he was a salty sailorman. I took it to show our friend, Teresa. She had asked me at one point who you look like. I answered, "Well, you never met my Dad. That's who he looks like." I decided to show her a picture. She said, "Oh, my gosh! That looks exactly like Josh." I said,

"He looks a lot like him for sure. Josh just has lighter hair and eyes." Grandpa was cute. Everyone always said so. You do look a lot like him. It was hard to tell after he got older and started wearing glasses and all, but in the pictures when he was young, the resemblance really shows. I have another picture of him with his brother. He is super cute in that picture, too. Maybe I will send that one to you later on.

Isn't it funny to see Grandpa hanging out with his buddies? He never talked about his buddies or the war. I don't know much about his time in the Navy. He really just loved being a husband and father. He was a quiet guy, who didn't say much, unless he needed to. He was always whistling and singing around the house. Grandma told me that when Grandpa was in the Navy, he had a hard time with all the guys around him cussing and swearing. He didn't like the way it sounded, so he decided to quit. When he married Grandma, he didn't think it was a good idea for his kids to see him drinking, so he quit drinking. I didn't see him drink even so much as a beer until I was about 19.

I was talking to Fino the other day. He has to get up and give a talk on what "manhood" means to him. He asked me what I thought he should talk about. I said, "What I know about manhood, I learned from my Dad. He believed morality, decency and commitment are everything. He lived clean and kept his word, to Grandma and to his kids, even his job. It seems so simple, but truthfully, it is very difficult. So many things pull in so many directions. Should I cheat here or bend the rules there? I don't know what made him able to do it." He wasn't raised well. He was sent off to relative after relative, he was beaten and ignored. He joined the Navy to escape his family. It's like all those "unsung hero" stories you read or hear about-- stories about common people, but Grandpa wasn't common at all. His job was common. His house and his cars, the neighborhood he lived in, they were all common, too. The man himself was not, but you already knew that. He lived his life in such a quiet way, the world will never fully know his impact. He raised Terry, Cindy, Gary, Leslie, Jimmy and Ruthie as if they were his own. (When my Dad married my Mom, she was a widow with 5 children. After all of us kids grew up, my parents adopted my little sister Ruthie) He even helped raise you. He wasn't trying to be a hero. He just liked doing it. He had made a promise, a commitment. You should be proud that you look like him. I know I'm really glad that you do. He was cute. So are you. Anyway, I thought you would like this picture. I sure miss you. I will visit in February. Until then, take care. I love you, Mom

Fire Crew #1

January 29, 2012

Hi Mom,
I know I haven't written in a while. I've been super busy with my fire fighter training. I finally graduated! I got a hat, blousers, a certificate and a picture of me and the training crew on the top of a lil' mountain with a cross and an American flag. It's pretty cool. Do you remember when we talked

about what crew I thought God would put me on? Well, it turns out that we had the same idea! I'm on Crew 1. I will be on crew by Wednesday of this week. Usually when you get on a crew, like anything else, you start at the bottom of the totem pole. However, I'm getting on and starting out as a second sawyer. I got hooked up. So that's what's going on with me lately, not much else. Oh, except I've started reading my Bible again. I just had the desire to. Mom, I must warn you. When it starts getting closer to fire season, I'm gonna be gone on fires a lot. When you come and visit, I might have to get up in the middle of it and leave. So your mission, if you choose to accept it, is to watch the fire weather conditions and look out for red flag warnings. LOL!

Hey, I almost forgot, Fino got approved to visit. I got the picture of Grandpa and his buddies. I wish he was still around. I miss him. Also, I received the letter about your new play. I thought it was very touching. I hope that it works out well for you. Love, Josh.

Mother's Day Play

I wrote a short play for the church. It was to be performed on Mother's Day 2012. I told Joshua about it and sent him a copy of the script. I used two of the letters I had received from him and combined them into one for a portion of the script. I even had Joshua's prisoner number on the costume of the young man playing the son.

"Never Alone"
Scene 1

Stage Right - Spotlight - The scene opens with a young man sitting on a prison cot writing a letter. He folds it, puts it in an envelope and seals it. Lights out.

Scene 2

Stage Left - A Mother walks to a mail box down stage, opens it and pulls out a letter. She holds it to her heart. She walks to a small desk up stage and sits down and begins to read it. (As she begins to read, the voice of her son speaks the words out loud. (Pre-recorded voice over.) The young man in the prison cell on the other side of the stage is low lit.

Dialogue

Dear Mom,

I feel so desperate. I'm trapped here in this place. I'm looked upon as unfit to walk among society and it's my own fault. I pray to God and ask for His forgiveness. I am not sure if He hears me. What is wrong with me, Mom? Why do I do things that lead to this? The other day I was thinking (I have lots of time for that now). Do you remember when we used to see the flocks of sheep? Well, I was reading a passage from Matthew 25:32. It talks about how Jesus will come back and shepherd his people. It made me think of all the open fields and how we used to see the shepherd with his flock and his little trailer and no matter what part of town and what road, he always seemed to be in a field near us.

Makes me wonder. Makes me think of my relationship with God. No matter where I go or what road I'm on, maybe He's always near, just waiting for me to come join his flock. Do you think He was trying to reach me, Mom? Can He really forgive me? Does He still love me? What about you, Mom? Can you forgive me? Do you still love me? I hope so. Sometimes I feel so alone. Love, Your Son

(The Mom takes out a piece of paper and a pen. She begins to write a letter. As she writes, she speaks the words aloud.)

Dear Son,

I received your letter today. I am so sorry to hear that you are in such a bad place. Even though you are older, my heart still sees the beautiful little boy with the sparkling eyes that occupied my days and nights for so many years. That boy should not have ended up where you are now. You see, I know your soul. I know who God created you to be. It's His gift to me, knowing my children.

To answer your question... Yes, if you ask, God will forgive you. And yes, He still loves you. Do I forgive you? Of course.

I must ask, please... don't let this happen again. You are at the very heart of who I am. I have been made strong and whole because of you. Today, I will give you the words I have prayed over you since the day you were born. They have been the silent cry of my heart. Now they belong to both of us. This is for you, my child. May you never feel alone.

(Song - At this point the Mother begins to sing a beautiful song about the way a mother's love follows her children throughout their life's journey. The Mom stands and moves forward. She begins to pray over the picture of her son. As she prays the lights come up on the prison cell on the other side of the stage. Jesus appears and tries to wrap his arms around the son. The son moves away... until, at the same moment, the praying Mom and the son drop to their knees. The son finally allows Jesus to wrap His arms around him and hold him. Lights out.)

*I chose to place the following letter out of date order, to share with you the church audience's reaction to the play. It was so powerful it became the deciding moment for me to write this book. Until I saw the impact the play had on the congregation at my church, I was unaware there were so many people who were dealing with the same pain and heartbreak I had experienced. I wanted to share the hope and redemption God had given Joshua and me with as many people as possible. Writing a book seemed a good way to do that. Please know that hope resides in God's loving arms and you are not alone.

May 12, 2012

Dear Joshua,
We did your play at church today. It was amazing! The
lights went out, and as the story unfolded, the room
became more and more silent. When the song had
finished, and the lights came back up, the only sound

123

heard was soft crying. Pastor Hennie took the plat-
form, but was so overcome with emotion that he could
not speak. We were all silent in the moment, realizing
God was speaking to hearts in a profound and deep
way. Pastor Hennie stood on stage and looked out at
the congregation as they wept. When he was finally
able to speak, he prayed... for sons and daughters to
be restored to their parents, for parents to be restored
to their children. I sat in the back of the room, tears
running down my face, yet smiling. I thought, "Look at
what Joshua has done." God has taken your mess and
made it a message for others. I was so proud. Proud of
the letter you sent that started it all. Proud of your abil-
ity to speak your heart so clearly and with such truth.
Proud that together we made a difference.

It sometimes seems you get a lot of attention for what
you do wrong, but not today! Today was a day of tri-
umph and celebration for what you do that is right and
good. It is more powerful and lasting than anything you
have ever done wrong. This was the best Mother's Day
I have ever had. I love you. Love, Mom

February 2, 2012

Dear Joshua,
I got your letter. It was a nice one--full of good news.
Congratulations on graduating! I'm proud of you! I'm
glad you got on the crew you wanted and that you are
second sawyer. God is good! Fino and I are going to try

to visit you on the weekend of Feb 11th. I'm glad you like the play for Mother's Day. It's really good, isn't it? I took actual words from a letter you wrote to me and fit them into the play. I think that is what makes it so good- -the realness of it.

Grandma called me and asked about the onions. You have to let them grow green stalks; then you pull them up and separate them by the stalks, cutting the bottoms apart before replanting them. You have to cut the stalks down to 1/3" so that more nutrients go into the onion and don't get wasted in the stalk. I had to look it up online. I have never planted onions.

Fino's son came to California to visit us. He painted the kids' classrooms at the church with graffiti letters that say "Rock Church" and "Faith" and "Hope." He used to tag illegally. Now he does it for God.

My theater arts program starts March 5th. It looks like it's going to be OK. Maybe if it goes big, we won't have to move in with Grandma. We can stay here instead. We'll see.

Hey, I'm glad to hear you are reading your Bible again. If you replace your thoughts with God's Word, it will change your outlook and by changing your outlook, you will change your life.

I will keep an eye on the fire/weather conditions this summer. That way I can better judge if I should come visit or not. Just make sure you stay safe while you're out fighting fires. You know how fire scares me.

Wasn't that a cool picture of Grandpa? It was BG--
before Grandma. Anyway, I need to close. I have to take
Squishee (the cat) to the Vet for the snip, snip. He has
matured nicely and I really don't want to deal with what
goes along with that. :) Have a good week. Stay safe
and warm and well. Love, Mom

I sent Joshua the pictures of my Dad as a way of reminding him that he was deeply loved. Growing up without a Dad was difficult for Joshua. The only male role model he had was my Dad. He taught Joshua how to use power tools and how to fish (Joshua still loves fishing). My Dad called him "Widdle Dods." It was like baby talk and it meant "Little Joshua." Josh thought my Dad was really funny. My Dad thought Joshua was sweet and gentle. They seemed to speak the same language. Near the end of my Dad's life, he developed Alzheimer's Disease. Joshua was middle school age. As my Dad's mind slipped away and he became more and more childlike, Joshua would spend time with him out in his garage, or in his tool shed keeping an eye on him while he tried to work. When I asked Joshua how he was able to handle that, he responded, "I just treat him the way he treated me when I was little." When he said it I went silent.

My Dad was right. Joshua is sweet and gentle. When my Father passed away, Joshua was very distraught. He came to the memorial service, but couldn't bring himself to walk into the church where it was being held. He couldn't face the loss. He has never visited my Dad's grave site at the Veterans Cemetery in Point Loma, California. He said, "I can't Mom. It's too painful."

I sent Joshua the pictures of my Dad when he was a young man, so Joshua could see that he belonged somewhere, that he was part of something bigger than himself. The proof was in the strong physical resemblance he had to my Dad. It's a good family line. It didn't start out that way. My Dad was neglected and abused by his parents, but he changed the trajectory of our family by raising seven children (6 of whom he adopted and raised as his own) with love and devotion. My children and I are the only family members from my Dad's blood line. He was deeply invested in the lives of his grandchildren as well. He left a proud legacy for us all. Joshua is a big part of that.

Squishee Made Me Laugh

After an attempt to visit Joshua, I wrote:

Dear Joshua,
Super upset right now... Fino and I came to visit you today, but it was the wrong day. I was all psyched up to see you and then when I got to the prison, they said I had to come back next Sunday. So I will see you next Sunday. Sorry.

I have enclosed your income taxes with a stamped, self-addressed envelope for each. Just sign them and send them in. The state will probably take all of your money, but you should get something back from the Feds. I wonder if you should leave it in your checking account to use when you come home. Maybe something to think about.

Things have been hectic around here. We have had some projects going on and then Fino's son came to visit and stayed a couple of weeks. He was stressed out and felt like he needed a break. The theater arts program that I am starting is getting closer and closer to the start date. I have been working really hard on it. I'm pretty stressed out myself! I'm having a really hard time with you being in prison. I am so tired of it. I don't like that you are being antagonized. I don't like that you are eating runny food. Gross! You could never keep weight on anyway. I'm worried you will waste away to nothing.

127

On a lighter note, my new little cat is so funny, nothing like Feats. He cries if he is not in the same room as me. Total baby. When I call him and he comes into whatever room I am in, he is a total maniac, biting me and attacking my feet and legs. He hardly ever wants to cuddle. Basically, he just likes sinking his teeth or claws into me. I can't really get him to play the way Feats used to play. Still, he purrs and keeps me warm at night. He likes to burrow under the covers. He'll sleep there all night. Today when I got back from trying to visit you, I was crying because I was really disappointed. I picked up the cat. I guess he didn't know what was wrong with me, so he tried to back away and started hissing at me. Stupid little cat! At least it made me laugh and cured my sad mood.

I will see you next week. I'm not sure about Fino. I don't know if he has somewhere he needs to be or not. He will probably come. He was looking forward to seeing you today. He had to wear his tan dress pants, because other than that, all he has is jeans. He didn't look like himself. Sorry I missed you this weekend. I will be there next Sunday. Love, Mom

I did go and visit Joshua the next weekend, and every other weekend after that. I wasn't receiving anymore letters from him. He was busy training to fight fires and working around the prison doing maintenance and repairs. Besides, I was seeing him so often there really wasn't much for him to write about that he hadn't already told me in person. On the weekends when we visited Josh, I would get really nervous. I was always worried that something would go wrong and I wouldn't get to see him. That actually only happened once, the day the fog came in. It was winter and a heavy fog was lying over the prison. If they can't see the inmates walking through the prison yard to the visiting center, they can't let them go. Makes sense. We had to wait for the fog to burn off. That took several hours. I only got to see Joshua for about 10 minutes. My Mom was with me. We were both very disappointed. There was one guard that seemed to be a nice guy. He apologized to us and said he would give us extra time before we had to check out.

Most of the guards didn't seem to care about the visitors. Others were downright mean. One in particular was so disrespectful that he would end up in a verbal confrontation with a visitor nearly every time I was there. I never said a word. I was concerned if I said anything they would take it out on Joshua. One time, that mean guard was yelling at the visitors as we were being processed. He was checking our shoes and wanding us with a metal detector and saying, "This is how it is when you come to prison folks." A sweet, little old lady finally responded, "I'm not in prison. I live on the free side." With that, the guard went silent and walked away. I guess he realized how ridiculous he sounded. Another time, he told me I had to wear my jacket buttoned up all day because I was wearing a tank top. My shirt had sleeves, but whatever. If I had to keep my jacket buttoned up to be able to visit with Joshua, then I would keep my jacket buttoned up. The entire time I was there, he would approach our table and lean in and look to make sure my jacket was buttoned. It was actually sort of funny. I kept thinking, "I don't break the law." It seemed that he assumed that if you were visiting someone in prison, you must be a law breaker, too. He had one more run in with some visitors shortly before Joshua came home. After that incident, I never saw him again. I always wondered if the prison staff had gotten one too many complaints about him and decided maybe he shouldn't be working with the public.

None of it really mattered. As I had told Joshua, "The guards are here for the long haul. They probably have car payments and house payments. They can't just walk away from their jobs. Even after this place is nothing more than an image in the rear view mirror for you, they will still be here. Don't pay too much attention to what they say is wrong. Just know that one day you will be home and they won't have any say in your life at all." Once Joshua came home, he realized that was true.

Stitched with Love

While visiting Joshua one weekend, he excitedly told me that he was out in an area for firefighting training where he and I had once hiked. When the other inmates on the bus with him realized he was familiar with the area, they began asking questions. In the same way he had become the carrot guru in county jail, he had become the guru for the local areas that the inmates visited while training or fighting fire.

When I got home from the visit, I wrote an email to my Pastor.

May 30, 2012

Hi again,
Almost 3 years ago, on a cool spring day, Joshua and I decided to go hiking. I wanted him to see the Santa Rose Plateau. Its beauty is good for the soul. The morning was clear, the sun was shining. We put on our hiking boots, grabbed some snacks and water, and headed out. We took the 15 freeway to the Clinton Keith exit and turned left. We drove down the winding, two-lane road to the plateau and pulled into the gravel parking lot. We talked and laughed as we headed toward the trail. We stopped at the map posted near the trail head. There are several hiking trails there. I decided, because I am not very familiar with the area, we should take a trail I had been on previously. It would take us to an old adobe house built when the area was first settled.

Off we went. We saw ground squirrels and hawks. We watched the grass on the rolling hills blow gently in the breeze. We talked about random unrelated things and also about my Dad. Joshua misses him a lot. We were enjoying the day when we reached the old adobe house. It was so cool! It had dirt floors and a wooden porch. You could look in the windows and see the small bedrooms, kitchen and sitting room. There were outbuildings, too. One must have been a small shed, but it had bars on the windows. Josh said it looked like a jail. There were tables for visitors to sit at and have a meal or a short rest. There was a large barn with a corral that led out to a large open pasture with a windmill. It was like walking into a time warp. We sat down and quietly took in the beauty of it all.

After awhile, Joshua looked up and said, "The sky is getting dark. Mom, I think it's going to rain. We should probably go." Joshua is always aware of his surroundings. I hadn't even noticed the dark clouds. We thought it might be fun to take a different trail on the way back. I thought I knew the right one. Turns out I was wrong. Although it was a nice hike filled with interesting sights, it didn't take us anywhere near the trail head where we had started. Fortunately, it did take us to the main road, so we could at least get our bearings. As we surveyed the area, I said, "My jeep is that way. We need to head back towards it." Joshua nodded in agreement. We headed in the direction of my Jeep. We had to stay on the trail as a small stream separated us from the main road.

We had walked only a short way when we felt the first few raindrops, and more followed. Soon, it was really pouring down on us. We tried to run, but that just got us wetter faster. There weren't even any large trees to hide *under. We were doomed! Then God sent us an angel. Well, he was actually a ranger, but he could very well have been hiding his wings under that khaki shirt! He was driving a pick-up truck and offered us a ride. Of course we said yes and jumped in. I sat in the middle between Josh and him. I told him that we had been out to the old adobe house but took the wrong trail back. He asked if we knew the story about the house. We said, "No." The ranger began to share it with us. The original house was built in the mid 1800's and was sold several times. By the 1900's, it was owned by a wealthy family and used for large social gatherings. One year some fireworks started a huge fire and one of the newer houses that had been built burned to the ground. There were no more parties or residents afterwards. Joshua was fascinated with the story. (And as it turns out, Josh was right about the building with bars on it being a jail. They used it to house drunken cowboys.) The ranger dropped us off at the trail head. We thanked him and got into my Jeep and went home.*

Now, back to the present day. Joshua called me last night. He was in a really good mood. He said, "Guess where I went today Mom?" I said, "Where?" He said, "The Santa Rose Plateau!" I responded somewhat surprised, "You're kidding me! Why were you there?" He told me they had to do a controlled burn to clear the area. He said they even parked in the same parking lot we parked in the day we went hiking. Josh and his fire crew hiked to the old adobe house where they sat down for lunch before starting their work. The crew was stunned by Joshua's knowledge of the area and the story he told of the house and the fire, the same story

*the ranger had told us. It's funny, but the men on Josh-
ua's fire crew always ask him where they are because
they know he is familiar with the region. I have taken
him from mountains to seashore, throughout San Diego
County, Riverside County and parts of Orange County,
in an attempt to show him that there is life beyond the
small neighborhood where he grew up. It seems God
honored that, because now he is considered the regional
guru of his fire crew!*

*While talking to him on the phone, I mentioned that
doing a controlled burn sounded dangerous and said,
"What if the wind changes direction or something?" He
said, "It did." He was the front man on the hose when
the wind changed and heard his captain shout, "Full
suppression." The fire was blowing back over onto the
men. Josh said the air was hot and black with smoke.
His face was covered with soot and ash. Tears ran down
his face and left tracks. His nose was running too. He
said he had "one foot in the black and one foot in the
green" (a phrase they use that means he was on the
front line). Then he added, "It was really fun!" Out loud
I said, "That would scare the crap out of me!" Josh
laughed and said, "Nah... it's fun."*

*After we ended our conversation (his allotted time on
the phone had run out), I started thinking about how his
life was so clearly being orchestrated by God. From the
heavens above, the hand of God reached down and with
a lovely golden needle picked up one side of the fabric
of his life, the day he and I went hiking, and delicately
stitched it into his present day circumstance so he could
find joy. Joshua really needed some joy.*

God never wastes anything--not a day or a moment. It all means something in His kingdom. And yesterday it was the gift of joy for Joshua, and by way of association, for me too. Gayle.

Bringing Joshua Home

Over the next year, I spent so much time visiting with Joshua in prison that I eventually stopped writing letters, too. We were talking in person; therefore, the letters became unnecessary. When Josh would get down because of being locked up, or because of an injustice he would experience in prison, I would always remind him that his circumstance was only temporary. He wouldn't be there forever, that one day the prison would be nothing more than an image in the rear view mirror. That would help him in the moment. Time moves quickly and I knew he could overcome if he could just get through the moment.

I sent my last letter to Joshua in March of 2013. In 4 months, he would be home. I shared with him my excitement regarding his homecoming and gave him a schedule of who and when we would be coming to visit. We could check off the visits as a way to mark time.

Joshua was incarcerated for 25 months. Near the end of June in 2013, he was released. For several weeks leading up to that date, there were threats from the guards to "give him more time no matter what they had to do," and constant worry that they would make good on those threats. There were questions about what county he would be released from and what time we should be there to pick him up.

He had me send him clothes to wear home. They call them" dress-outs." I had to mail them to the prison in a specific size box, a specific amount of days prior to his release, and write his name, prisoner number and the words "dress-out" on the label. He was very worried that the clothes wouldn't get to him on time. He knew that I had saved all his clothing, so he sent me a letter listing the items he wanted me to send:

> Pants-jeans
> Shirt - ?
> Belt - black
> Boxers - clean

I laughed and thought, "Does he really think I would send him dirty underwear?" In preparation for his home coming, I bought a wall decal and placed it in the archway between our living room and family room that read, *"There's no place like home."* I bought a new bedroom set, bedding, curtains, pictures, and then readied his room. I washed all of his clothes that had been boxed up and stored away, and filled his closet and dresser. As I stood back and looked at the completed work, I realized all that was missing was Joshua. At the grocery store the week before his release, I bought extra food so I could prepare his favorite meals. He had eaten jail house slop long enough!

The day arrived. My stomach was in knots as I showered and dressed! My husband and I got into our car and drove the 30 minutes to pick up Joshua. We went to the visitor's center at the prison, the same place we went to check-in for visits while Joshua was locked up. They told us that we needed to wait in the first parking lot, the one we had just driven past. We drove back to the lot and waited for hours.

He was supposed to be released in the morning. It was after 12pm before we finally saw the white van full of now-free inmates make its way towards us. I was so anxious and excited that I started to shake. I opened the car door and got out before the van even reached us. I was so ready for this. The van pulled up and stopped. The side door slid open. Several men who weren't my son got out first. I strained to see Joshua. And then there he was, smiling as he stepped out of the van. He only made it halfway to our car before I ran to meet him and wrapped my arms around him. Through tears I said, "Finally." He replied simply and gently, "Don't cry, Mom." I tried for his sake to put on a brave face. It almost worked. We loaded up his few belongings and got into the car. Then, as I had said to Joshua so many times before, the prison became nothing more than an image in the rear view mirror, small and powerless. Before us was the road home. We were taking Joshua home! And we all know, there's no place like home.

Once Joshua was home, there was a period of adjustment for him. In a half hour drive, he went from being inmate number F95736 with no freedom, living in a cell on a bunk surrounded by hundreds of other men, to simply being Joshua, with every freedom imaginable, his own room with a soft mattress, and the focus of his parents' love and forgiveness. On occasion, he found it emotionally overwhelming. Still, he was joy-filled and seemed to treasure every moment. I surprised him by bringing his dog to our house. Louie and Joshua both jumped and howled upon seeing each other again!

Going to the grocery store was a thrill for Joshua. He would say, "Mom, let's go to the grocery store." It was always after I had worked 8 hours and was tired. I would reply, "Josh, I'm tired. I don't really want to go." He would plead, "Please Mom! It's my favorite thing to do. In prison, you don't have any choices. There are only 3 kinds of everything: soap, socks, and cookies; but here on the outside, there are so many choices!" I would buckle under his logic and end up going with him. Joshua felt the time we spent shopping together was also a way for us to bond and create shared memories. He loves me and from that love came the desire to share the things that brought him joy. Seeing Joshua so happy made me happy, too. He would "peruse" (as he called it) the aisles, picking up random products and inspecting them, sometimes placing them in his shopping cart and sometimes putting them back on the shelf. And we had to go down every aisle! It took hours, but Joshua could always make me laugh and no matter how tired I was, the outings to the grocery store always proved to be fun.

Josh went to work for one of his friends, a guy he had known since high school, who had actually taken time away from his family to go visit Joshua in prison. (Chris, if you're reading this, Thank you from the bottom of my heart.) He paid Joshua a decent wage and had him build a retaining wall at his house among other miscellaneous work. It kept Josh afloat until he was able to find a real job.

We also had a great summer. Joshua missed the ocean while he was locked up, so one of our first outings was to the coast in North San Diego County. He stood and watched the waves crash, drinking it in like a thirsty man. He breathed in the salt air and let it fill his lungs.

He also wanted to see our family. His Grams, his nieces and nephew, his step-brother Nick and his sister and her husband. He said while he was in prison with only pictures to look at, he felt like everyone had died. He said, "All I had were pictures, Mom. Like when you lose someone and you never get to see them or hear their voice again. It was like they had all died. I missed them so much. I never want to be away from my family again."

He came to church for the first time on the 4th of July holiday weekend. I found it interesting and timely that we were celebrating freedom. For Joshua it held special meaning. I cried when I saw him walk into the building. I was singing and had to be there early to rehearse, so my husband ran to the house and picked him up. They did it on the down-low, so I would be surprised (I'm so blessed by the men who love me). I was singing the Battle Hymn of the Republic with two of my closest friends. I felt the power of the words, "Mine eyes have seen the glory." It seemed a miracle that my son was in church with me.

In all honesty, I thought I would have buried my son by now, that he would not have lived to see 30, but God was stronger and He saved Joshua. I had been fearful that prison would destroy him. God knew better and it was the very thing that saved his life. And through Joshua's redemption, God also healed me. As my son learned the power of forgiveness through Christ, he was able to forgive me. There is no perfect parent and I certainly was not one, but with Joshua's undeserved love, devotion and forgiveness towards me, all of the guilt, doubt and fear that I felt over his addiction fell off like chains.

And so it was that God had done a mighty work, not just for Joshua, but for me as well. As I looked back over the years Joshua and I spent battling his addiction, I realized that in the darkest moments, when our very lives were threatened, and all hope seemed lost,

God was with us. We were never alone. As the years slip by and my son and I draw nearer to eternity, we know (John 8:36) "whom the Son [Jesus] has set free, is free indeed!" May you find your freedom, too. Love, Gayle

Acknowledgements

*Thank you all for encouraging me and taking time out of your
already busy lives in order to be a part of this book.*

Fino Garcia
Jennifer Romero
Lucinda Mileski
Rene Stephens
Maui Arumbulo
Mark Mikelat
AJ Twiss
Elizabeth Kelly
Grace Spina
Ranee Alison Spina

And of course, Joshua

About the Author

Gayle Garcia has worked in the Creative Arts Ministry for many years as a recording artist, worship leader, and playwright. It was not until her faith was tested through the harrowing journey of helping her son become free of addiction to drugs and alcohol that her writing turned towards this very personal story.

Gayle now speaks to various groups and shares her story of the trials faced, and the lessons learned during her son's recovery. Her life is now dedicated to encouraging others facing seemingly insurmountable circumstances. Through the healing POWER of God's love, and the confidence in believing that God is faithful, Gayle inspires us all.

To contact Gayle about speaking engagements or interviews, or to purchase the book in quantities for group workshops, please visit:

www.NeverAloneBook.com